The Doctrine We Adorn

The Salvation Army

THE
DOCTRINE
WE ADORN

International Headquarters
London

Printed in Great Britain
by
THE CAMPFIELD PRESS, ST ALBANS

GENERAL ORDER

This book contains an abridged study of the basic doctrines of The Salvation Army as set forth in the Salvation Army Act 1980, Schedule 1.

A more detailed study is given in The Salvation Army Handbook of Doctrine (1969 Edition).

The 11 doctrines are to be taught in connection with the training of all Salvation Army officers.

All Salvation Army teaching, whether in public or private, must be in keeping with these 11 Articles of Faith.

International Headquarters
London

'. . . adorn the doctrine of God our Saviour in all things'
(Titus 2:10).

CONTENTS

THE RELIGIOUS DOCTRINES OF
THE SALVATION ARMY

(As set forth in the Salvation Army Act 1980, Schedule 1)

1 We believe that the Scriptures of the Old and New Testaments were given by inspiration of God, and that they only constitute the Divine rule of Christian faith and practice.

2 We believe that there is only one God, who is infinitely perfect, the Creator, Preserver, and Governor of all things, and who is the only proper object of religious worship.

3 We believe that there are three persons in the Godhead—the Father, the Son and the Holy Ghost, undivided in essence and co-equal in power and glory.

4 We believe that in the person of Jesus Christ the Divine and human natures are united, so that He is truly and properly God and truly and properly man.

5 We believe that our first parents were created in a state of innocency, but by their disobedience they lost their purity and happiness, and that in consequence of their fall all men have become sinners, totally depraved, and as such are justly exposed to the wrath of God.

6 We believe that the Lord Jesus Christ has by His suffering and death made an atonement for the whole world so that whosoever will may be saved.

7   We believe that repentance towards God, faith in our Lord Jesus Christ, and regeneration by the Holy Spirit, are necessary to salvation.

8   We believe that we are justified by grace through faith in our Lord Jesus Christ and that he that believeth hath the witness in himself.

9   We believe that continuance in a state of salvation depends upon continued obedient faith in Christ.

10   We believe that it is the privilege of all believers to be wholly sanctified, and that their whole spirit and soul and body may be preserved blameless unto the coming of our Lord Jesus Christ.

11   We believe in the immortality of the soul; in the resurrection of the body; in the general judgment at the end of the world; in the eternal happiness of the righteous; and in the endless punishment of the wicked.

PREFACE

THE word 'doctrine' means 'teaching', a word often found in the New Testament (eg, Matthew 7:28; Mark 4:2). Christian doctrine is, therefore, the teaching of Christian truth.

In the study of doctrine we can go only as far as that which God has made known. We are limited also by what our human minds can understand and what our language can explain of the mysteries of divine truth. At best we can know only 'in part' (1 Corinthians 13:9).

Our spiritual condition is also important in the study of doctrine, for it is the spiritually-minded who understand spiritual truths. It is as we do God's will that we prove the truth of the doctrine (John 7:17; see also Matthew 6:22, 23; John 14:17; 2 Corinthians 4:4, 6).

The Salvation Army's Articles of Faith are in general agreement with evangelical Christian teaching based on the Bible.

Note: A glossary is included which will explain the meaning of some of the words used in these studies.

The words 'man' and 'mankind' are used to describe the human race.

1

The Bible as the basis of Christian doctrine

'We believe that the Scriptures of the Old and New Testaments were given by inspiration of God, and that they only constitute the Divine rule of Christian faith and practice' (Article 1).

Section I. Introduction

This is the first of the 11 statements of Salvation Army belief because all we accept as doctrine comes from the Bible.

We claim that God Himself authorized our teaching because He makes known, through the Bible, those truths which are important to our salvation. Our doctrines are based on these truths alone.

Section II. Why we obey the Bible

The Bible contains the writings of the Old and New Testaments. The word *Bible* comes from *biblos*, a Greek word meaning 'book'. The Bible is the greatest of all books. By calling it the Holy Bible we mean that it has been given by God for His holy purposes. The Bible is both a book and a collection of books like a library. It is the written record of God's message to mankind and is, therefore, also called Scripture (meaning 'writing').

1   *What kind of authority does the Bible have?*

The authority of the Bible rests on the strength of its claim that its writers were inspired by God (see section IV). Through its writings God has made known Himself and His way of saving mankind.

This claim is strengthened by the testimony of the Christian Church through 20 centuries, and by the fact that millions of believers, of all races, have proved the truth of its teaching in their lives.

No subjects are more important than those with which the Bible deals. The Bible tells of God, the Creator of all things, and of His will for mankind. It shows how we can be made free from sin and receive power to live a Christlike life. It tells of the world to come and of what will happen finally to the saved and to the unsaved.

We can use our minds and learn much about ourselves and the world in which we live. We may also become aware that God exists. But we cannot know all the truth about God's nature and purpose unless God makes Himself known as He does in the Bible. The Bible tells us that 'God was in Christ, reconciling the world unto himself' (2 Corinthians 5:19).

William Booth wrote that the Bible is 'the only authorized and trustworthy written revelation of the mind of God. In this it stands alone . . .' (see section III).

Concerning Christian faith and conduct the Salvationist does not accept any other writing or authority as equal to the Bible.

2   *Christian creeds and traditions*

The Salvation Army's Articles of Faith are in general agreement with truths contained in the ancient Christian creeds known as the Apostles' Creed and the Nicene

Creed. These creeds are not substitutes for the Scriptures, from which they take their authority, yet they state clearly the important truths of the Christian faith.

We do not, however, accept without question all that some Christians believe and do by tradition or custom. While we respect the views of other Christians, we do not accept that all the traditional beliefs and practices which have developed in the Church since New Testament times are necessarily binding upon us.

3   *The meaning of faith in the study of doctrine*

The word *faith* means more than the *act of believing* (see Articles 7 and 8). When we refer to the 'Christian faith' or 'the faith', in studying this Article, we mean those truths or doctrines which we believe. This is what Paul meant in 1 Timothy 4:1 and 6:21.

Doctrines are brief statements of those Bible truths which are necessary to Christian life. These doctrines, however, may be held in the mind without making any difference to one's daily living. It is most important, therefore, that the Christian commits himself fully to God in keeping with his personal faith in these truths. Then the Holy Spirit, who inspired the Bible writers, will come into the life of the believer and will:

- *(a)* strengthen his belief that the Bible comes from God and that its teaching is true, and
- *(b)* work within his life to translate these truths into positive Christian living, which we know as the spirit of salvationism.

Section III. The meaning and nature of revelation

Revelation' is the 'unveiling' or making known of that which has been hidden.

3

1   *Divine revelation*

Is God making known the truth about Himself and His will for mankind. This revelation is of two kinds:

(a) General or natural revelation by which we may learn something about God and His truth as we think about:

> (i) The work of God *around us* in nature which shows His wisdom and power.
>
> (ii) The work of God *within us*—giving to us the knowledge that we depend on God and the feeling that we must obey and answer to Him.
>
> (iii) The work of God *in history* where we can see what happens to people and nations when they disobey God's laws (Proverbs 14:34; Galatians 6:7).

(b) Special or supernatural revelation which God gives directly to man. This is recorded in the Bible.

It is because natural revelation does not tell us all we need to know about God and His will for mankind that we need the special revelation found in the Bible.

2   *How God gave His special revelation*

God's special or supernatural revelation .was given through chosen people and in different ways (Hebrews 1:1, 2). He revealed His truth, more and more, over hundreds of years as His people were able to receive it.

It was given in early times to Abraham and his descendants, the people of Israel, who were specially chosen to receive, guard and record the truths they received.

Both prophecy (telling forth) and miracle (special acts of God) played an important part in all this. God spoke through the prophets of Israel, showing Himself as Lord of history. Miracles were signs of His power and authority (Hebrews 2:3, 4; Acts 14:3).

God's greatest and most complete revelation came, however, in His Son, Jesus Christ, of whose life, death and resurrection the Gospels tell. In and through Him, most of all, God's power was shown (see Acts 2:22).

3   *Divine revelation gave to mankind, down through the years, a growing and deepening knowledge of:*

- (a) *What God is like*—His love, His power, His justice and His mercy (Hebrews 1:2, 3).
- (b) *How God expects us to behave* in the world (see Mark 12:28-33 and Matthew 5:21-48).
- (c) *His plan for our salvation* (see Luke 24:25-27, *New English Bible,* and 1 Peter 1:10-12).
- (d) *Life after death* (compare Isaiah 26:19 and Daniel 12:2 with Luke 20:37, 38 and John 11:23-26; 14:1-3; see also chapter 10).

4   *Jesus Christ is God's greatest revelation to mankind*

- (a) *The most important features* were Christ's perfect oneness with the Father, and His sinlessness (John 1:1; 10:30; 1:18, *New English Bible*).
- (b) *This revelation came through Christ's character, His teaching and His work.* His sacrifice on the Cross showed most clearly the love and the holiness of God (1 John 4:9, 10).
- (c) *The revelation through Christ was taught by the apostles.* The book of Acts and the Epistles explain what the life, death and resurrection of Jesus mean for us and show how we can follow His teaching.

5

(d) Jesus Christ is clearly the central Person in the Bible. He is the One to whom Old Testament revelation pointed and from whom all later revelation comes (John 16:12-24).

Section IV. The inspiration of the Bible

1   *What is divine inspiration?*

  (a) 'Inspiration' means 'breathing into'. By divine inspiration of the Bible we mean that the Holy Spirit 'breathed into' or guided God's chosen servants who then made known the truth they received (2 Peter 1:21).

  (b) This inspiration does not mean that God always gave to Bible writers the exact words they used in the Bible. The Holy Spirit revealed truth in many different ways to different people. Each of God's messengers gave his message in his own way, while the Spirit caused him to see that God was speaking even through the *events* of his time.

  (c) God's purpose was to make known to mankind the way of salvation through Jesus Christ and to teach us how to love and serve Him (2 Timothy 3:15-17, *New English Bible*; John 20:31).

2   *Evidence that the Bible is inspired by God*

  (a) Evidence in the Bible

    (i) The wonderful unity of the Bible points to the fact that the one God must have inspired its 40 or more authors. Its 66 books were written over a period of 1,500 or 1,600 years. In them almost every form of literature can be found—law, history, parable, poetry,

6

prophecy, proverb, life stories and letters, all have a place. Amongst its writers were soldiers, politicians, kings and peasants, prophets and priests, fishermen and shepherds. Yet the Bible is a unity as it tells and explains God's revelation to mankind. The central theme is Jesus Christ. The Old Testament prepared for Him; the New Testament shows how He more than fulfilled the hopes of the Old Testament.

(ii) Jesus often spoke of the Old Testament writings as having come from God (John 10:35; Matthew 21:42; 22:29, 31).

(iii) New Testament writers believed in the divine inspiration of the Old Testament and often quoted from its pages (eg, the Acts and the Epistle to the Hebrews).

(iv) Old and New Testament writers claimed that their words were given by God (Exodus 34:27; 1 Corinthians 2:13; Revelation 1:17-19). The phrase 'Thus saith the Lord' is found before many Old Testament messages.

(b) Other evidence

(i) Bible writers were so sure that God had spoken to them that they risked persecution or death in giving their message (Jeremiah 20:8, 9; Acts 7:51-60).

(ii) The fulfilment of prophecies and of promises given in God's name show that they come from God.
    The history of the Jews and their survival as a race continues to be the fulfilment of

God's covenant with Abraham (Genesis 17:1-8).

Jesus and His Church also fulfil Old Testament hopes and prophecies—a powerful witness to the divine inspiration of these writings.

(iii) The Bible meets the deepest needs of all people. A large part of the world has been completely changed by the Bible's high standards of purity, truth, justice and mercy. This is especially true of the teaching of Christ.

(iv) Those who accept and follow Bible teaching know that the Bible is inspired by the witness of the Holy Spirit in their hearts. Believers can say, 'I know that the Bible is inspired because it inspires me.'

3   *The Bible and scientific knowledge*

The Bible is not a textbook of human knowledge or of the history of the universe. The increase of scientific knowledge does not affect its truth or authority. The Bible tells of the creation of the world by God, its dependence on Him, His work in the world and His care for all He has made.

Section V. How our Bible came to us

1   *The Canon of Scripture*

The word 'canon' comes from a Greek word meaning a 'rule' or 'measuring stick'. The *Canon of Scripture* is the list of 66 Old and New Testament books which the Protestant Church believes to be the God-given rule for Christian faith (doctrine) and conduct.

The Old Testament is the Christian term for the Jewish Scriptures. These have their origin and authority in the covenant or agreement made between God and Israel through Moses. 'Testament' means 'covenant'.

The New Testament is the Christian term for the written record of the 'New Covenant' promised in the Old Testament (Jeremiah 31:31-34) and fulfilled in Jesus Christ (Mark 14:24). (See also Hebrews 8:6, 7, 13.)

2   *The Old Testament*

These 39 books (Genesis to Malachi) were accepted by the Jews into their Canon of Holy Scripture in three stages—the *Law,* the *Prophets* and the *Writings.*

(a) *The Law,* sometimes called the *Pentateuch* (meaning 'five books' in Greek), consisted of Genesis, Exodus, Leviticus, Numbers and Deuteronomy. These were accepted by about 400 BC.

(b) *The Prophets* consisted of the *'Former Prophets'* (Joshua, Judges, Samuel and Kings) and the *'Latter Prophets'* (Isaiah, Jeremiah, Ezekiel and the 12 'minor prophets'—so called because they were shorter writings). The '12' were Hosea, Joel, Amos, Obadiah, Jonah, Micah, Nahum, Habakkuk, Zephaniah, Haggai, Zechariah and Malachi. These gained general acceptance by about 200 BC.

(c) *The Writings* refer to Psalms, Proverbs, Job, Song of Solomon, Ruth, Lamentations, Ecclesiastes, Esther, Daniel, Ezra, Nehemiah and Chronicles. These were accepted as part of the Jewish Canon by about AD 90.

3   *The Christian attitude toward the Old Testament*

The Old Testament spoke of people's need and hope of

a Saviour, but the New Testament is the record of these being fulfilled in Jesus. This is made clear in the Epistle to the Hebrews.

The 'Old Covenant' called for obedience to written rules which had no power to change human lives.

The 'New Covenant' is good news (the gospel) because it offers every believer a new relationship with God through faith in Jesus Christ. Nevertheless the Old Testament is a necessary part of our Bible because it prepares the way for the New.

4   *The New Testament*

The 27 books of the New Testament were written after Jesus came into the world. They were soon seen to be of greatest importance, by Early Christians, in teaching them what to believe and how to act.

The four *Gospels* were written to meet the need for a record of the life and teaching of Jesus.

The *Epistles* were letters written by church leaders to advise the young churches on particular problems of belief and conduct.

These writings were collected and used for the teaching of new converts. They also found an important place in church services along with the Old Testament Scriptures.

Early Church Councils confirmed these writings which had already been accepted by general use and which agreed with the true teaching of the first apostles.

Other writings were not included because they did not have true authority. The 27 books, now known as the New Testament, had become part of the Canon of Scripture by about AD 367. Their strongest authority, however, is in the truths they contain.

Note: The division of the Bible text into chapters and verses came much later in AD 1551.

2

God

'We believe that there is only one God, who is infinitely perfect, the Creator, Preserver, and Governor of all things, and who is the only proper object of religious worship' (Article 2).

Section I. Introduction

It is not possible for a human person, who is limited, to fully understand God, who is unlimited (see Isaiah 46:5; 1 Timothy 6:15, 16). Our knowledge of God is limited to what He chooses to reveal of Himself and human words are not good enough to express even this.

Nevertheless God wants us to know Him, and in Jesus He has revealed Himself so that we might respond, in loving obedience, to His holy love (John 1:14; Colossians 2:9; Hebrews 1:2, 3).

Section II. The attributes of God

1 *What is meant by 'attributes'?*

In the Bible there are many statements about the special qualities which mark the nature (character) of God. These are called His attributes, and the statements about them help us in three ways:

11

(a) They show that God has certain powers and qualities which belong only to Him.

(b) They give clear reasons why we should give Him our respect, yet also our trust.

(c) They help to correct mistakes in the way we think about God.

We must remember that God's various attributes are all together in His nature which cannot be divided.

2 *Attributes of God as a divine Person*

(a) *He is personal*—that is to say, God is not some *thing* like a power or influence. He is some *One* whom we may know as Father (see section V.2*(c)*).

(b) *He is Spirit.*
We are not to think of Him as having a bodily form. Yet He is no less real to us. When Jesus said, 'God is Spirit', He was teaching that God is not limited to time and space as we are and that He can be approached by worshipping hearts everywhere (John 4:21-24, *New English Bible*).

(c) *He is eternal and not created* (Psalm 90:2).
He has neither beginning nor ending. His being and powers do not depend on any source apart from Himself. This is what God meant when He said to Moses, 'I AM' (Exodus 3:14).

(d) *He is unchanging* (James 1:17).
God's nature, being perfect, does not change, yet it is expressed in many different ways.

(e) *He alone is God* (Isaiah 45:5).
He is above all created things. Nothing is outside the scope of His rule.

(f) *He is One, yet Three-in-One.*
This doctrine is dealt with in section V.

3   *Attributes concerned with God's power*

  (a) *He is present everywhere (is omnipresent)* (Jeremiah 23:23, 24).

  (b) *He knows everything (is omniscient)* (Psalm 147; Hebrews 4:13).

Nothing is hidden from Him or is beyond His understanding. He knows Himself (1 Corinthians 2:11) and He knows the creation He controls (Luke 12:6, 7).

Unlike human knowledge which is limited to what is known of the past and present, He knows all the possibilities of the future as well (Isaiah 46:9, 10). Man, who lives in space and time, cannot understand the experience of God who is eternal and not so restricted.

  (c) *He can do all things (is omnipotent)* (Genesis 17:1; Matthew 19:26).

There is no limit to God's power. He can do all He wills to do in keeping with His nature. His 'purpose is everywhere at work' (Ephesians 1:11, *New English Bible*). All power within His creation comes from Him and no being could exist without Him.

This, with God's other attributes, means that all things are subject to His presence, His knowledge and His power.

4   *Attributes concerned with God's nature*

  (a) *He is holy* (Leviticus 11:44; 1 Peter 1:16) (see chapter 9, section II, paragraph 2).

This means that:

    (i) He hates and is separate from all that is evil and is pleased with all that is good.

(ii) All mankind, being unworthy in the light of such holiness, should 'stand in awe of Him' (Psalm 33:8) and give Him due worship.

(iii) He wants us to be holy and is able to make us holy, so that He can live within us and use us for His glory (see chapter 9).

(b) He is love (1 John 4:8).

We see this:

(i) in His goodness to all He has made (Psalm 145:9). He cares for evil persons as well as the good; the unjust and the just (Matthew 5:45);

(ii) in His teaching against all kinds of selfishness, which works against love; and

(iii) most of all in His work of saving mankind from sin (see 1 John 4:8-10).

God's love is of a different quality to human love and only He can reveal its truth and meaning to us. God loves us in spite of our sin (Romans 5:8, 10) and His love shines strongest when it is most tested.

Yet it is wrong to think that, because God loves us, He must approve of our way of life. God's loving desire for us is that we should become His children (see 1 John 3:1-3, *New English Bible*). This is a gift to be received (verses 1, 2) and a high standard to be reached (verse 3).

Section III. God as the Creator, Preserver and Governor of all things
(See Genesis 1:1; Isaiah 45:12; Romans 11:36, *New English Bible*)

1 *These three words, 'Creator', 'Preserver' and 'Governor', should be thought of together*

Together they teach us:

(a) that God is not only Creator of all things, but that He keeps and controls His creation which depends on Him in order to exist. 'All things' means the whole universe (see Colossians 1:16);

(b) that God is Preserver and Governor of spiritual as well as material things. We may therefore know Him also as a wise, holy and loving Father (see paragraph 5); and

(c) that there is meaning and purpose in all that God has made.

2 God as Creator

By His power He brought into being everything that exists apart from Himself.

(a) He brought into being all that science has discovered and may yet discover.

(b) He works within His creation and controls it, yet is separate from it. He has made it known that His creation is not yet as He wants it to be (Ephesians 1:9, 10; 2 Peter 3:13).

3 The presence of evil in creation

(a) Despite the fact that God is Creator, we know that evil is present in His creation in many different forms. This leads us to ask two important questions:

    (i) Did God, who is perfect in every way, create evil things also?

    (ii) If God has power to do all things and is a righteous Governor, why does evil have such power in the world?

(b) These are proper questions. The short answer is that evil has no place in God's Kingdom (Genesis

1:31). The presence of evil in the world and God's action against it is dealt with in all our other Articles. God's complete power over evil and His action to expel it from His Kingdom is one of the Bible's main themes.

4   *God as Preserver*

  (a) God takes care of all creation by His power (Isaiah 40:25, 26).

  (b) He provides all that is needed for life and its support (Genesis 8:22; Psalm 145:9, 15, 16; Acts 17:25, 28).

  (c) He cares even for those who rebel against Him (Matthew 5:44, 45).

  (d) This care depends on man co-operating with God.
If we are lazy and careless we will suffer loss and we cannot blame God for this. God also expects us to love and help others in need (1 John 3:16, 17). Many people suffer need because they have been forgotten, not by God, but by man (Isaiah 3:14, 15; Matthew 25:42-45).

  (e) God's greatest provision is His offer of salvation (2 Peter 3:9). No one lives by bread alone and our spiritual needs are of first importance (Matthew 6:33).

  (f) God's love reaches out in a special way to those who, through obeying Him, suffer hardship.
He enables them to triumph over their hardships (Psalm 121:7; Romans 8:31-39).

5   *God as Governor*

  (a) He rules over creation by means of the laws of nature.

(b) He rules over man who is subject to this 'natural law' for his material needs, as well as to the 'spiritual law' of God's Kingdom as a child of God.

Section IV. God is the only proper object of religious worship

1 *God is the only One we should worship because He alone is God* (Exodus 20:3; Psalm 96:5, 8, 9; Matthew 4:8-10)

(a) Religious worship is given to a god. Jesus taught that we should worship only the one true God (Matthew 4:10). Such worship can be in many different ways so long as all are directed to God 'in spirit and in truth', for 'God is spirit' (John 4:24, *New English Bible*).

(b) The commandment 'Thou shalt have no other gods before Me' was given to *correct* religious ideas and practices already held by men. Man is a worshipping creature and will worship other objects if not shown the way to the true God. This wrong kind of worship not only dishonours God but harms the worshipper. Reference is made in Romans 1:18-32 to the effects of such worship.

(c) Believers must therefore guard against the kind of worship which falls short of what God requires, such as:

  (i) worship that depends wholly on form or ceremony;

  (ii) worship that leads our thoughts away from God to something or someone else, being only a part of His creation.

17

This failure to understand that God is separate from and greater than His creation causes many people to worship places, objects or persons having no right to such honour (see Acts 3:11, 12; 10:25, 26; 14:13-15; Romans 1:23, 25; Revelation 22:8, 9).

The New Testament sees these practices and attitudes as being like idol worship. Nothing must be given the place that belongs to God alone (Colossians 3:5; Matthew 6:24).

(d) Those who worship the true God should also witness to those who do not (see Romans 10:12-17). Examples of such witness may be found in Acts 14:13-17 and 17:22-31.

2 *We worship God because He alone is God and because of what we know of His power and perfections*

(a) Our worship will therefore include:
  (i) respecting Him because He is God;
  (ii) thinking of Him as Creator and Preserver;
  (iii) obeying Him as Governor;
  (iv) loving Him for His goodness.

(b) We worship best when we honour God for what He is, asking for no more than the privilege of fellowship with Him.

(c) True worship is worship with our whole being. 'Thou shalt love the Lord thy God with all thy heart, and with all thy soul, and with all thy mind, and with all thy strength' (Mark 12:30).

Section V. The Trinity

'We believe that there are three persons in the Godhead—the Father, the Son and the Holy Ghost, undivided in essence and co-equal in power and glory' (Article 3).

1   *Our third Article refers to the triune (three-in-one) nature of God*

This doctrine comes from the New Testament revelation. This revelation teaches that there is only one God (Mark 12:29; 1 Corinthians 8:4) but that God is Three-in-One (a Trinity)—Father, Son and Holy Spirit.

2   *Basic truths about the Trinity*

  (a) *The titles Father, Son and Holy Spirit belong to the three Persons in the Trinity and are not shared or exchanged with one another.*

  (b) *These three Persons are, nevertheless, one undivided whole.* God is Father, Son and Holy Spirit.

  (c) *We may speak of God the Father, of God the Son, and of God the Holy Spirit.* Each Person is fully divine, sharing equally divine power and glory.

The word 'person' is not able to fully explain the Three-in-One nature of God. No language can supply an exact word to mean all that the truth contains. We can only say that the Father, Son and Holy Spirit are each personal to us—yet they are not three but one Person (see also chapters 3 and 4).

3   *How these truths about God were made known to men*

Men learned of the triune God through their own experience and from history over a long period of time.

19

God's continuing revelation of Himself came in three important stages:

(a) *Through Israel*—that which was recorded in the Old Testament concerning the one true God who is Lord of creation. As time passed He would make known more and more about His nature, His presence and power.

(b) *By Jesus.* Those who accepted Jesus as truly God and truly man also came to believe that:

   (i) although a separate Person from the Father who sent Him, Jesus was one with God in a Father-Son relationship (John 10:30; 14:10, 11);

   (ii) *Someone* would take His place and be always present *within* them—the Holy Spirit or the Comforter, a separate Person from the Father and the Son, but also *one* with them (John 14:16; 16:7).

(c) *To the early disciples at Pentecost.* They had seen and known God in Jesus and now experienced His Spirit living within them, as Jesus had promised. Therefore they were led to give divine worship to the Father, Son and Spirit. Yet they had no doubt they were worshipping the one God who made Himself known to their forefathers.

Thus the doctrine of the triune God came from Christian belief in God the Father and Creator who, in Jesus, had come to dwell with men, and who was now ever present, by the Holy Spirit, in the hearts of His people (see Acts 2:33, 36; 4:24-30; 5:30-32; 7:55-57, 59, 60; 15:28).

4   *These three stages in God's revelation can be seen in the way our Articles present the doctrine of the Trinity*

(a) *This doctrine is necessary for salvation.*

Without its truths the gospel cannot be preached or understood. We need to know that the work of the Son and of the Holy Spirit for our salvation (see Articles 4 and 6-10) are truly acts of God (see Article 3).

Thus God fully shows His divine nature.

(b) The Trinity is eternally at work in every act of God.

The Scriptures tell us that God the Father, God the Son and God the Holy Spirit are equally at work in creation, as in all divine actions in the world. Yet each has His special ministry (see paragraph 7).

(c) The doctrine of the Trinity has to do with what God is as well as what He does. This truth is stated in our third Article.

5 *The mystery of the Trinity cannot be fully explained by means of pictures or likeness to material things*

However, the three-in-one nature of God has been partly illustrated by:

a plant having leaves formed by three leaflets; the human person having mind, feeling and will; water in the form of ice, liquid and steam, and in other similar ways.

6 *We can learn much from the Bible about the Trinity*

These truths were made known most of all through Jesus:

(a) By the teaching about Jesus:

(i) *At His birth* (Luke 1:35) *and baptism* (Matthew 3:16, 17).

(ii) *In the words of John the Baptist,* showing the important link between the baptism of Jesus and Pentecost (John 1:33).

21

(iii) *In the writings of the apostles* who saw also that in Christ the hopes of the Old Testament came true, eg, Acts 2:34; Hebrews 1:8, 9.

(b) By what Jesus Himself said:

The promises He made (see John 13-16) are seen to have come true, and His prayer (John 17) answered in the Acts and the Epistles:

   (i) Spiritual life came to believers and the Church was born (Acts 2:32, 33; 1 Peter 1:2).

  (ii) The message of salvation was made known and proved (Hebrews 2:3, 4).

 (iii) The work of the atonement became effective (Ephesians 2:18; Titus 3:5, 6).

 (iv) God's power came into human lives (Ephesians 3:14-19).

  (v) Christians were made able to work and witness for God (1 Corinthians 12:4-7).

7   *We need to know that each of the Three Persons has His own special work*

(a) Article 3 follows Christian practice in naming the Father as the First Person, the Son as the Second Person and the Spirit as the Third Person of the Trinity.

(b) The Father is known as the First Person because it is from Him that all else comes.

   (i) He is the Father of all mankind, for He created and cares for them (Ephesians 4:6).

  (ii) He is Father in a closer sense to those who have become part of His spiritual family, through believing in the Son (John 1:12; Romans 8:15).

(c) The Second Person is the Son, sent from the Father, who came to earth in human form and gave Himself for the salvation of the world (John 3:16) (Articles 4 and 6).

(d) The Holy Spirit is the Third Person whose power is seen in the lives of God's people, making them strong for service. His ministry is explained in chapter 4.

(e) Yet the whole Godhead (Father, Son and Spirit) is involved in all divine acts (see 2 Corinthians 5:19; Ephesians 3:16-19).

(f) The relationship of the Three is shown by referring to the Son as *born* of the Father (His only Son, John 3:16) and to the Spirit as *proceeding* (or coming) from the Father and from the Son (Acts 2:33).

8   *The word 'God' is mostly used for the Trinity as one, or for the First Person in the Trinity*

When speaking of the Son or the Spirit we generally say, 'God the Son' or 'The Son of God'; 'God the Holy Spirit' or 'The Spirit of God'.

Prayer is addressed usually to the Father, in the name of the Son, through the Holy Spirit. Prayer can also be made to the Son or to the Holy Spirit.

9   *The right way to approach the doctrine of the Trinity is:*

(a) To keep in mind the basic teachings from which it comes:

that there is one God;
the Father is God;
the Son is God;
the Holy Spirit is God.

23

The Three are separate Persons, yet they are One. This is the fullness of God.

(b) To see the doctrine as part of the gospel message which says that God comes to each of us personally, in all His fullness, to bring us salvation.

(c) To recognize that we cannot know everything about God, for our human language is not able to explain Him. Our limited minds cannot fully understand the divine mystery, for nowhere in creation can we find anything to which He can be likened.

3

Jesus Christ

'We believe that in the person of Jesus Christ the Divine and human natures are united, so that He is truly and properly God and truly and properly man' (Article 4).

Section I. Introduction

1   *This statement about Jesus Christ should be thought of along with the rest of our doctrines*
It is closely linked with His saving work for mankind (Articles 6-10) and with the Christian doctrine of the Incarnation as stated in John 1:14. 'Incarnation' means 'becoming flesh', from the Latin word *carnis,* meaning 'flesh'.

The statement that Jesus is truly God unites this Article with Articles 2 and 3.

2   *These two most important truths are made known in the New Testament*
  (a) *We are told of Christ's early life.* The four Gospels tell of His birth, His words and deeds, His death, resurrection and His ascension.
  (b) *We are shown these events in the light of eternity.* We learn that Jesus is the Son of God who became man and, by His saving work, carried out God's plan of salvation (see especially John 16:28; 17:4, 5; Philippians 2:6-11).

25

3   *Our beliefs about Jesus Christ must include the truths that:*

  (a) His divine nature is eternal (John 1:1-4; Revelation 1:4).

  (b) He became truly human, being born of Mary by the Holy Spirit. He lived on earth as a man yet He was truly divine (Luke 1:30-35).

  (c) Because of this He could offer Himself as the divine Atonement (Article 6).

  (d) His human nature did not come to an end when He went back to Heaven. In His glory He is still *one* with mankind, acting as Saviour because of His incarnation and saving work on earth (Articles 7-10) (1 Timothy 2:5; Hebrews 2:11, 17, 18).

  (e) He will be made known to all in His divine glory (see Article 10).

  (f) His coming again will mean the end of sin and the final salvation of the faithful who are watching for Him (Hebrews 9:24-28).

4   *All these statements go together*

The truth about the person of Jesus Christ is linked with His mission to the world.

Section II. His manhood

1   *Jesus is truly human* (Hebrews 2:16-18).

  (a) *This truth puts away any idea that the Eternal Son, who came to earth, only seemed to be a man.* Such errors as this arose in New Testament times (see 1 John 4:2, 3).

  (b) *Jesus was truly man on earth because this was God's will.* To carry out God's purpose it was

necessary that His divine Son should become a man in every way (Hebrews 2:17). It was made known to certain persons that He would be a man of special character with a special work to do (see Matthew 1:19-21; 2:2; Luke 2:13-17, 28-33).

Also people came to know, from what He said and did, that Jesus was no ordinary person (see Matthew 16:13-16). Yet they knew that He was indeed a man (John 7:46; Acts 2:22).

(c) The New Testament makes this truth clear:
   - (i) *Jesus spoke of Himself as being man* (John 8:40).
   - (ii) *John the Baptist and the apostles called Him a man, even when speaking of His deity and glory* (John 1:30; Acts 2:22; Romans 1:3).

2   *The New Testament shows that Jesus had to depend, during His earthly life, on such help as is available to everyone*
   (a) His body was human. He *hungered* (Mark 11:12), *ate* (Mark 2:16), *thirsted* (John 19:28), became *tired* (John 4:6), *slept* (Matthew 8:24), *wept* (John 11:35) and *died* (John 19:30).
   (b) His feelings were human. He felt joy and sorrow and showed approval or disapproval of what He saw, in ways that we can understand. He spoke of the things that moved Him to pity or that made Him angry (see Luke 13:10-17; Matthew 18:21-35; Luke 10:29-37; 15:11-32).
   (c) His mind was human.
   - (i) *His mind developed as He grew in body* (Luke 2:52).
   - (ii) *He learned facts as we do* (Mark 11:12, 13; Mark 6:38; 8:5; John 11:34).

(iii) *He was sometimes surprised*—showing that His knowledge was limited (see Matthew 8:10 and Mark 5:9).

(d) He lived as one of the people, sharing their problems. He was helped by His Jewish religion and by the blessings of home and human friendships. He had to bear with those who wished to harm Him and was affected, as others, by the social conditions of His time.

(e) He was tempted as we are tempted (Hebrews 4:15).

The Gospels show that He knew temptation from the beginning to the very end of His life (see Luke 22:28). He was tested in every way and had to choose between God's way and the easier way (Mark 14:36). In this He is one with us.

(f) He needed and used the spiritual help available to His fellow men.

He worshipped in the home, the synagogue and the Temple. He studied the Scriptures and, above all, lived a life of prayer. Prayer was necessary for Him, whether amongst the people (John 11:41, 42) or alone with God (Mark 1:35; 6:46; Luke 5:15, 16).

By living close to God he found guidance and the strength to carry out God's will, even to Gethsemane and the Cross.

3   *Jesus became a man so that He might be one with mankind for ever*

He both shares human experience and is the perfect example of manhood.

(a) The Son of God took upon Himself the title 'Son of man' to show that He is one with the whole

human race. Their lost condition is His concern, whatever the cost, and He shares their sufferings (see Acts 9:4; Matthew 25:44, 45).

(b) Jesus became God's true pattern for manhood. Although He was human like ourselves (Romans 8:3) and was tempted as we are tempted, yet He was 'without sin' (Hebrews 4:15; see also 2 Corinthians 5:21 and 1 Peter 2:22).

In the light of the gospel we see the truth that God wants us all to be like Jesus. He is God's ideal and has opened the way for all to be 'truly human' according to God's plan.

Section III. His divine nature

1   *We may learn about the divinity of Christ from:*

(a) *His own teaching* (see paragraph (d)(i));

(b) *His character and His miracles* (Acts 2:22);

(c) *His Incarnation, Resurrection and Ascension and the powerful things done in His name by His followers;* and

(d) *the teaching of the New Testament.*

     (i) *The Gospel of John* (see especially chapter 20:28-31). In this Gospel we read of what Jesus Himself said about His divine link with the Father and with the Holy Spirit.

    (ii) *The Epistle to the Colossians,* written to show that Jesus is the only Saviour we need (see especially Colossians 1:12-22).

   (iii) *The Epistle to the Hebrews,* written for Jewish Christians to show how Jesus fulfils the hopes expressed in the Old Testament about the promised Messiah.

29

2   *Other New Testament statements speak directly of the relationship of Jesus with the Father*

At the baptism of Jesus a voice from Heaven said:

> 'Thou art my beloved Son, in whom I am well pleased' (Mark 1:11).
> (See also Mark 9:7; John 1:1; 5:23; 10:30; Acts 20:28.)

3   *Jesus is stated to have those powers and perfections which belong only to God* (John 14:9; 16:15; Colossians 2:9).

   (a)   *He is holy* (Hebrews 7:26; Revelation 3:7).

   (b)   *He is love* (John 15:9; Ephesians 3:19).

   (c)   *He lives for ever* (John 1:2; 8:58; Revelation 1:11, 18).

   (d)   *He has all power* (Omnipotence) (Matthew 28:18; Philippians 3:21).

   (e)   *He is present everywhere* (Omnipresence) (Matthew 18:20; 28:20).

   (f)   *He knows everything* (Omniscience) (Colossians 2:3).

   (g)   *He does not change* (Hebrews 13:8).

4   *Jesus has done and will do that which only God can do*

   (a)   *He was one with the Father as Creator, Preserver and Governor* (John 1:3; 1 Corinthians 15:24; Colossians 1:16, 17; Hebrews 1:13).

   (b)   *In matters of human conduct He acts:*

      (i)   *as Lawgiver* (Matthew 5:28, 32, 34, 39, 44; also 7:24, 26).

      (ii)   *as Judge* (John 5:22; Acts 10:42).

(c) In spiritual matters He:
- (i) brings God and man together (John 1:29; 6:51; Hebrews 1:3). (See also chapter 6, section I, paragraph 2, and section III, paragraph 1*(a)*.)
- (ii) gives the blessings which come from this union (Matthew 9:2, 6; John 11:25, 26; 17:2; Acts 2:33).

5   *Jesus is shown as receiving worship as God*
- *(a) From His followers* (John 20:28; Acts 7:59; John 9:35-38; Revelation 1:5, 6).
- *(b) From angels* (Hebrews 1:6; Revelation 5:11, 12).
- *(c) From all creation* (Philippians 2:9-11; Revelation 5:13).

6   *Jesus made claims that can rightly be made only by God*

(See references in preceding paragraphs to His own words, eg, John 11:25, 26. See also John 14:10-14.)
- *(a) He claimed to be one with the Father* (John 10:30; 14:9).
- *(b) He accepted worship as God* (Luke 24:52).
- *(c) He said that the Father Himself would testify* to the truth of the claims He made (John 5:36, 37; 7:16, 17; 8:18 etc).
- *(d) These claims were made at the risk of His life and led at last to His death* (John 5:18; 10:33; 19:7).

7   *The Old Testament speaks of the truth about Jesus*

Of these Scriptures Jesus said, 'they . . . testify of Me' (John 5:39). We may find this witness frequently in the text of the New Testament.

The truth about Jesus is shown to be the highest point of Old Testament history and the fulfilment of its teaching (see Luke 24:44-47; John 5:45-47; Acts 2:16-21 etc). This is the special message of the Epistle to the Hebrews.

Section IV. The divine and human natures united in His Person

1 *In the Lord Jesus Christ the divine and human natures are united in one Person*

He is not two Persons, one divine and one human; neither is He part divine and part human as a divided Person.

This statement will help us to understand the truth expressed in Article 4. When we speak of Jesus as God, we still know that He is truly man. When we speak of Him as man we remember that He is truly God.

2 *When God the Son became a human being, it meant for Him a giving and a humbling of Himself*

(See 2 Corinthians 8:9; Philippians 2:7, 8.)

3 *God's purposes for mankind through the In-carnation were carried out by means of the human limitations accepted by Jesus*

There was no other way for God to show His self-giving love and His great desire to bring men into a living fellowship with Himself.

Jesus won the victory over evil by the power of holiness, love and truth.

Because He is both God and man, the Lord Jesus Christ is:

32

(a) The One who, more than any other, has shown us what God is like (Hebrews 1:3).

(b) Our Brother and Helper showing human sympathy and divine power (Hebrews 4:14, 16).

(c) Our Advocate and Saviour by whom we are restored to God's favour:

    (i) United with God and mankind He has opened the way for everyone to have fellowship with God and with one another (Galatians 3:28);

    (ii) By His life and death He leads us to repentance and saving faith (see chapter 7, sections II and III);

    (iii) In the power of His risen life He lives in those who receive Him, enabling them to live victoriously.

4   *Though Jesus was human, the teaching He gave was true and reliable*

He grew in knowledge and in spirit by means available to everyone. He used His mind, studied the Scriptures and, through prayer, was constantly in touch with His Father God. He grew in spiritual life by living in God's light and learning from Him (see John 3:11-14).

He did not claim, as man, to know everything (Mark 13:32), but He knew all He needed to know for His saving work, having learned from God (see John 5:20; 6:46; 8:14).

He claimed that His words were eternal truth (Mark 13:31) and that they were approved by the Father and the Holy Spirit (Luke 9:35; John 14:26; 16:14; see also Matthew 7:24, 25).

Section V. His names and titles

1 *Each of the names and titles given to Jesus shows some truth about Him*

No one name or title gives all the truth, so names and titles are often used together as in 'The Lord Jesus Christ'. The word 'Lord' points to His divinity, 'Jesus' to His humanity and 'Christ' to His work or mission.

These three truths about Jesus are seen in the various other names and titles given to Him.

2 *Those which speak of His divinity*

   (a) The Son of God

      This title shows Jesus within the Trinity. His special right to this title is clearly marked in the New Testament (see John 3:16; Romans 8:3, 32).

   (b) Lord

      This title points to His divinity and His right to receive worship (Philippians 2:10, 11).

   (c) The Word

      This is a translation of the Greek word *logos,* but does not give its full meaning (see John 1:1, 14 and Revelation 19:13). *Logos* is used in referring to Christ before He 'became flesh' (the Incarnation). The meaning includes God making Himself and His purposes known. Probably the best explanation is found in Hebrews 1:1-3.

When Jesus is called 'The Word', the meaning includes *all that He is, all that He does* and *all that He says.*

3 *Those which speak of His humanity*

   (a) Jesus

      This is His name as man. It is an ordinary Jewish

name, but it was specially chosen because it means 'Jehovah is Saviour'. Thus it describes His mission to men (Matthew 1:21).

'Jesus' is also the New Testament form of 'Joshua'.

(b) *The Son of David*

This was one of the titles given to the expected Messiah or King (see Matthew 21:9; Romans 1:3; Luke 1:32; 2:4).

(c) *The Son of Man*

This title shows that Jesus is human like ourselves and one with every 'son of man' of every race. He is the triumphant Son of man who will 'come in the glory of His Father' (Matthew 16:27) as Judge, King and Lord. He will call all people to answer for the way they have lived (Matthew 25:31-46).

4   *Those which speak of His work or mission*

(a) *The Christ*

'Christ' is the Greek word for 'Messiah' or 'Anointed One' (John 1:41). See also Peter's words in Acts 2:36.

(b) *Saviour* (Luke 2:11)

In the Old and New Testaments God was known and called upon as Saviour (Isaiah 43:3; Titus 1:3). New Testament teaching shows that each Person of the Trinity works for our salvation (Titus 3:4-6).

(c) *The Servant of God*

There are many references in the Old Testament to the 'Servant' of God who would suffer and die in carrying out God's plan of salvation (eg, Isaiah 42:1-4; 49:1-6; 50:4-9).

35

Matthew's reference (12:18) to Isaiah 42:1 shows Jesus as the Servant of God.

Other names given to Jesus, such as Emmanuel ('God with us'), the Lamb of God and the Good Shepherd, picture other truths about Him and His mission.

4

The Holy Spirit

Section I. Introduction

The person and the work of the Holy Spirit are spoken of in Articles 3 and 7, but other Articles also relate to the doctrine of the Holy Spirit. This doctrine includes His *place as the Third Person of the Trinity,* His *work in creation,* the *record of what He has done* (especially linked with the life and teaching of Jesus) and His *presence at Pentecost and in the world today.*

Section II. The Holy Spirit in the Godhead

1   *Article 3 states that the Holy Spirit, as Third Person in the Trinity, is equal in power and glory with the Father and the Son*

In the Bible the Holy Spirit is given divine names and titles. He is shown as having divine powers and as receiving worship.

2   *The Bible teaches that the Holy Spirit is a Person in the same sense as the Father and the Son are Persons*

  (a) The word for 'spirit' in Greek and Hebrew also means 'wind' and 'breath'. The power of the Holy Spirit is sometimes likened, in the Bible, to the force of a 'wind' or 'breath'. However, it is important to remember that the work of the Spirit is that of a divine Person.

  (b) *Jesus taught this very clearly,* speaking of the Spirit working as a Person along with the Father

37

and with Himself (John 14:16, 17, 26; 15:26). He spoke of the Spirit as 'the Comforter', 'the Spirit of Truth' and 'the Holy Spirit'.

(c) We read of the Holy Spirit as a Person,

  (i) *knowing* (Romans 8:27; 1 Corinthians 2:10, 11),

  (ii) *feeling* (Ephesians 4:30),

  (iii) *deciding* (1 Corinthians 12:11) and

  (iv) *taking action,* such as hearing, speaking, guiding and giving.

3 *The Bible teaches that the Holy Spirit is truly God*

  (a) The Spirit is shown as being one with God.
  (Compare Isaiah 6:8-10 with Acts 28:25-27, where the words of the Lord in Isaiah are quoted in Acts as being the words of the Holy Spirit.)
  The Spirit within us is God within us (1 Corinthians 3:16).

  (b) The Holy Spirit, being God, is:

  (i) present everywhere (Psalm 139:7-10),

  (ii) all-knowing (1 Corinthians 2:10, 11),

  (iii) love (Romans 5:5; Galatians 5:22).

  (c) He is to be worshipped because He is divine (Matthew 28:19; 2 Corinthians 13:14).

  (d) To disobey the Holy Spirit is to disobey God (see Ephesians 4:30; Acts 5:3, 4; Matthew 12:31, 32).

Section III. The work of the Holy Spirit

1 *Every act of God is the work of the Holy Spirit*
He is the Spirit of life and light, eternal, all-powerful and ever-present, who is working always in holy love.

2   *The Bible shows us that the Spirit works:*
  - *(a)* in a general way in the lives of all people as, for example, in making the sinner aware of his sin. He also chooses and prepares certain persons for special tasks;
  - *(b)* in every part of our lives—body, mind and spirit— and in our relationships with others.

Thus we see that the Holy Spirit's work is not always out of the ordinary or miraculous, as some may think.

3   *The Holy Spirit was at work in Old Testament days*
  - *(a)* *He prepared men to carry out the special duties to which they were called,* for example:
    - (i) Moses and those who helped him (Numbers 11:17).
    - (ii) Bezaleel and his tabernacle workers (Exodus 31:1-6).
    - (iii) Gideon and David (Judges 6:34; 1 Samuel 16:13).
  - *(b)* *He inspired the prophets to give out their messages* (Micah 3:8; Peter 1:21).
  - *(c)* *He made people aware of their need to be right with God* (Psalm 51:9-11; 143:10).
  - *(d)* *Old Testament writers promised:*
    - (i) that the Spirit of God would be upon the coming Messiah (Isaiah 11:1, 2; 42:1; 61:1);
    - (ii) that the Spirit would be poured out on all mankind (Ezekiel 36:26, 27; Joel 2:28-32).

4   *The Holy Spirit was at work in the life and ministry of Jesus*
  - *(a)* *In the message to Mary* (Luke 1:35).
  - *(b)* *When Jesus was baptized* (Matthew 3:16).

(c) *In the wilderness* (Matthew 4:1).

(d) *In the teaching of Jesus and of John the Baptist* (see Luke 4:16-21; Matthew 12:28; John 1:33; 7:37-39; 15:26).

Section IV. The ministry of the Holy Spirit

1   *The presence and power of the Holy Spirit are necessary to salvation*

Jesus taught His disciples that His work on earth would be carried on by the Spirit. He promised that the continuing presence of the Holy Spirit would make up for any loss they would feel when He was no longer with them in human form (John 16:7).

2   *The New Testament shows the Holy Spirit to be specially linked with truth, holiness and power*

(a) He is called 'the Spirit of *truth*' (John 14:17). He causes us to see things as they really are. Thus:

    (i) He enabled New Testament writers to understand *the truth* about Jesus (John 15:26, 27; 16:12, 13) and to write it down under His guidance.

    (ii) He makes known to sinners *the truth* about sin and that Jesus is the only Saviour (John 16:7-11).

    (iii) He makes God's people sure of *the truth* about their salvation and sanctification (see chapter 7, section VII).

(b) He is 'the *Holy* Spirit'. This reminds us that all true goodness or holiness in men comes from Him. It is He who produces the 'fruit of the Spirit' in human lives (Galatians 5:22, 23).

(c) He is the giver of *power* for Christian living and service (see Luke 24:49 and Acts 1:8). Paul preached in the '*power* of the Spirit' (Romans 15:19).

3 *The Holy Spirit brought the Christian Church into being*

(a) God works out His purpose for the world not only through chosen persons but also through a chosen race or people. In Old Testament times the people of Israel served this purpose. Today the Christian fellowship, which is the Church, has the responsibility. The Church is a fellowship of those whom God has called together in Jesus Christ whatever their race or nation may be (Galatians 3:28; Ephesians 2:14; Colossians 3:11).

(b) The Church is helping to bring about God's eternal purpose to 'gather together all things in Christ' (Ephesians 1:10). It came into being:

    (i) *by the calling and training that Jesus gave His disciples;*

    (ii) *by Christ's saving work* (Acts 20:28; Ephesians 5:25);

    (iii) *by the Holy Spirit's coming upon the first disciples and upon those who believed 'through their word'* (John 17:20; Acts 2:38, 39, 41, 42, 47).

(c) The Holy Spirit's work amongst the fellowship of believers was:

    (i) to set up the Christian Church and help it to grow, and

    (ii) to control and use this spiritual fellowship for the spreading of the gospel throughout the world.

Christ's promise that 'the Holy Spirit . . . will teach you everything' (John 14:26, *New English Bible*) and 'guide you into all truth' (16:12-14) came true when, for example, His early followers gave us the books of the New Testament. These serve the Church as 'the Divine rule of Christian faith and practice' (Article 1).

The Spirit also gave the first Christians power and guidance as they took the gospel message to other lands (see Acts 1:8; 2:4; 4:29-31 etc).

4 *The Holy Spirit still works in human lives in these ways and amongst the Christian Church as a whole*

  (a) He is concerned with our relationships with God, with other people and with our fellow Christians.

  (b) He calls, appoints and prepares Christians to serve the Church and to be spiritually nourished by it (see Romans 12; 1 Corinthians 12; Ephesians 4: 1-7).

     The gifts of the Spirit enable Christians to serve in different ways (1 Corinthians 12), but the greatest need is shown to be love (1 Corinthians 12:31; 13:1; Ephesians 4:2).

  (c) He calls, appoints and prepares Christians to be witnesses for Christ to the world. This witness is to be given not only through preaching, but also through the power of Christian living (1 Timothy 1:15, 16) and Christian fellowship (John 13:34, 35).

  (d) He causes Christians to be concerned about the needs of others (Luke 10:36, 37; 1 John 3:16-18). Salvationists should be witnessing and caring people whose hearts are open to the working of the same Holy Spirit who led and empowered their fathers in the faith.

(e) His work of grace in each life is done only by that person's consent. The Bible warns, therefore, that the work of the Spirit can be hindered, His appeals resisted and even refused. We are commanded to 'receive' the Spirit (Galatians 3:14), to be 'filled with' the Spirit (Ephesians 5:18) and to 'walk in' the Spirit (Galatians 5:16, 25).

5   *Other New Testament passages which deal with the work of the Holy Spirit are Galatians 5:16-25 and Romans 8:1-27*

Both passages deal with the Spirit's work in the human soul and speak of Him as the source of holiness of heart and life made possible by the Atonement.

Further teaching about the Holy Spirit is given in chapters 7, 8 and 9 of this handbook.

5

Man's special abilities and sinful state

'We believe that our first parents were created in a state of innocency, but by their disobedience they lost their purity and happiness, and that in consequence of their fall all men have become sinners, totally depraved, and as such are justly exposed to the wrath of God' (Article 5).

Section I. Introduction

The main truth stated in this Article is that all men are sinners. (The words 'man' and 'men' are used to describe every human person.)

While the Article refers to man's fall into a state of sin for which he must face God's judgment, we should keep in mind that sin is not part of God's will for man. Sin came in because of man's disobedience and the remedy is found in God's saving work through Christ.

God shows mercy with His judgment.

Section II. Man's special abilities

1 *Although man is connected with the world in which he lives, he is also separate from it*

The Bible shows him to be the highest part of God's creation. Man is more than a natural being; he does not 'live by bread alone' (Luke 4:4). God has made him a spiritual being with a special place in the divine purpose for the world. Man therefore has dignity and value of his own.

These truths about man having both a lowly and an exalted state are given throughout the Bible (see especially Psalm 8 along with Hebrews 2:5-11).

2   *The special gifts which set man above the rest of God's creation are his ability to reason, his sense of right and wrong and his spiritual nature*

(a)   *Man is one person, having body, soul and spirit* (1 Thessalonians 5:23).

His body links him with the natural world, while his spirit is that eternal part of him by which he can enjoy a fellowship with God. The word *soul* is sometimes used for spirit or to mean all that is not of the body. It can also refer to the whole person.

(b)   *Man has powers of reason* by which he can think and plan in a way unknown to the animal creation.

(c)   *Man has moral powers,* a sense of right and wrong. Thus he knows how he ought to behave towards other people (see paragraph 3).

(d)   *Man has spiritual and religious powers*—the desire to seek and worship God and to respond to what He makes known.

(e)   *Man can make progress* and improve himself as he uses his powers. He reaches his best when dealing with things which are of eternal value. He finds deepest satisfaction in the right use of his best powers (Matthew 16:26).

(f)   *Man's natural gifts are harmed by his sinful state* (see section VI, paragraph 2), especially when they are used for unworthy purposes.

3 *Man's moral powers can be seen in the way his conscience works, for he is free to choose*

  (a) The working of conscience.

      According to spiritual light received man has a sense of right and wrong and knows that certain actions and attitudes are either good or bad. There is an urge within him to do what he thinks is right and not to do what he feels to be wrong. His conscience judges his conduct, approving or condemning him as the case may be (see Romans 2:14, 15, *New English Bible*).

      While sin harms man's moral powers and makes him less able to do what is right, God still speaks to the weakened conscience and His saving power can bring healing and restoration.

  (b) Freedom of choice.

      Man has no choice in such matters as his birth and the natural laws by which he lives. In other ways, however, he is free to act according to his conscience or desire.

      God has given and respects this moral freedom but man is still responsible to God. Man can choose to disobey God's law, but he cannot avoid having to answer to God for his decisions (Galatians 6:7, 8).

4 *Man has to live among other people*

His life is bound up with the lives of others on whom he must depend and whom he must serve. His life and person are influenced by the past and the present, while he in turn can influence the present and future welfare of others.

    God deals with men as separate persons, but always as persons who have a relationship to Himself and to others (see Matthew 22:36-40).

Section III. The proof of man's sinful state

1   *The Bible speaks of men as sinners*

  (a) Every man is seen as a sinner in need of salvation
  (see Romans 3:23; Isaiah 53:6; 1 John 1:8, 10).

  *(b) Human sinfulness is revealed most of all by the
  teaching, life and death of Jesus.*
  In His *teaching* Jesus spoke about sinful desire
  (Matthew 5:28), sinful acts (Matthew 18:6) and
  sinful neglect (Matthew 25:41-43, 45), all of which
  are against the law of love. Thus He showed how
  far men fall short of God's perfect will.
  By His *sinless life* of love Jesus gave an example of
  what God wants us to be. So we see how different
  our lives are from His pattern of manhood.
  His *death* caused by men points to man's sinfulness. His willingness to die on the Cross for our
  sins shows how terrible sin must be in God's sight.

  (c) Human sinfulness is proved by human experience.
  The inner voice of conscience rebukes us when we
  do what we know is wrong (John 8:9; 2:15).
  Examples from history show what great harm and
  loss have been caused by men's wrongdoing. Laws
  and punishments have been made necessary to
  keep them from harming one another.

2   *The Bible shows how men live and act in ways that
are against the will of God*

Human sinfulness is:

  (a) Against God's eternal purpose for man (Genesis
  1:26, 27, 31; Ephesians 1:4; 2:10).

  (b) Not in keeping with the example given by Jesus.
  God's actions against evil and His purpose to
  destroy it are clearly shown in the Bible and

most plainly in its teaching about Christ's saving work.

Section IV. The fall of man

1   *The Bible teaches that sin began when God's gift to man of freedom to choose was misused*
We read of Adam and Eve falling to Satan's temptation and disobeying God's command (Genesis 3:3, 6).

2   *The story of the fall of man teaches certain truths about life and history*
   (a) *We all come from the same first parents.*
       'God hath made of one blood all nations of men' (Acts 17:26) and all may share the blessings of the family of God (Ephesians 2:17-19; Galatians 3:28).
   (b) *Man is not now the same as when he was created.*
   (c) *Man has faced and fallen to temptation since history began, with unhappy results for himself and his descendants.*

   These important truths are strongly confirmed by the teaching of Jesus.

3   *Only through the right use of his freedom to choose could man have made moral and spiritual progress*
His disobedience in turning away from what is good robbed him not only of the blessings he had (sinlessness and fellowship with God) but also of those he might have gained through obedience. The way of free choice by which he could have reached his goal became the cause of his downfall. Thus we see that, where there is great possibility for good, there is also the same possibility for evil.

48

4 *This third chapter of Genesis teaches that, throughout history, men have been deceived by thinking:*

  (a) That happiness comes when a man can do as he likes without hindrance and without having to answer for what he does (Genesis 3:4, 5; see also Galatians 6:7, 8).

  (b) That man can reach a worthy goal while disobeying or ignoring God.
  Thus man chooses a wrong goal (see *(a)* above) or a wrong way to reach the goal (see *(b)* above).
  Sometimes he is tempted to try to do the right thing by a quicker or easier way than God's way (see Genesis 3, where Eve is seeking knowledge, and Matthew 4:1-11, where Jesus wants to fulfil His mission).

  (c) That God is unworthy of man's respect and worship.
  In Genesis 3:4, 5 the tempter is suggesting that God is untrue and cannot be trusted. This kind of thinking harms relationships between man and God and destroys desire for spiritual fellowship with Him.

Section V. The nature of sin

1 *Sin is anything that is not in keeping with the will of God*

It is sin that comes between man and God. Many different words are used for sin in the Bible, but no word by itself can show how wrong sin is. Therefore we need to explain any word we use, for there are different kinds of sins (see section VII).

2   *Sin is that which is judged to be sin by God*

We sometimes judge others wrongly by our own ideas of what sin is. We may also approve of that which is sin in God's sight (Luke 16:15).

Jesus had to tell the Pharisees that they were wrong in their conduct and teaching (Matthew 15:3, 9). Sin is that which displeases God and breaks His laws.

3   *God makes known His will for us in different ways*

It is made known through *natural* revelation (Romans 1:19, 20) and through *conscience* (Romans 2:14, 15). More knowledge of God's will and His nature is found in *the Bible* through the Law, the Prophets and most of all by Jesus. This knowledge is strengthened by the Holy Spirit's work in each life and within the Church.

4   *When we understand God's will and His laws, we also become aware of our own sinfulness*

   (a) *When we know God's standards we realize how far short we fall of them.*

   Thus the law shows to us our need of salvation. It reveals sin but cannot cure sin (Galatians 3:24).

   (i) *It is wrong therefore to think that salvation comes through keeping the law* (Romans 3:20).

   (ii) *It is also wrong to ignore God's law and pretend that sin does not matter.*

   God wants to show us what is wrong and our need of a cure for sin.

   (b) *The greatest light comes from Jesus, and none who has knowledge of Him can accept any other standard as God's will for man.*

   The light of Christ's example causes the sinner either to turn away, wanting the darkness, or to cry, like Paul, 'What shall I do, Lord?' (Acts 22:10).

(c) In this light we see that selfishness is the root cause of sin.

Self takes the place which belongs to God, and selfishness becomes the rule of life instead of love. This self-centredness can poison human relationships and spoils even those acts which would otherwise be good and acceptable (Matthew 6:1-5).

Section VI. The effects of sin

1   *Sin causes spiritual separation from God*

Sin is more than the breaking of certain rules; it is fighting against what we know to be God's will. In so doing we separate ourselves from God in whom is found true life. This is the real harm that sin causes to the sinner (see Ezekiel 14:7, 8; Jeremiah 2:13).

There is, however, a sense in which the sinner cannot remove himself from the love and lordship of God. Man has to depend on God for the very powers he uses against Him.

The story of the prodigal son (Luke 15:11-24) shows the result of this wrong use of the blessings God gives. Disaster came to the son and grief to the father.

2   *Spiritual separation from God brings spiritual loss and weakness in facing evil*

(a) The sinner loses the blessings which come only from fellowship with God.

To turn aside from the Giver is to lose His gifts. When we lose the protection of God's grace, we cannot resist evil and our nature comes under its power (see James 1:14, 15; Timothy 2:26).

(b) The corruption of sin affects every part of our being. This is the meaning of the words, 'totally depraved'.

The whole life is affected because the *heart* has been corrupted (Proverbs 4:23).

The *mind* is darkened, so that it cannot understand spiritual things (1 Corinthians 2:14; Ephesians 4:18; 1 John 2:11). The *will* is weakened by the pressure of sinful desires. The *conscience* becomes hard, so that its warnings are no longer heeded (1 Timothy 4:2).

Yet the sinner can still reason and respond to what is good. He can still become aware of the foolishness of falling into sin and an awakened conscience can rise in protest against it. Jesus said that evil men may yet respond to good as well as bad desires as, for example, in family life (see Luke 11:11-13).

3   *Sin can make us slaves* (Romans 7:19).

Every time we sin the habit is made stronger and we come more and more under its power (John 8:34). We can never free ourselves without God's power (Acts 26:18).

4   *Separation from God is spiritual death*

This is a truth which affects this life (see Ephesians 2:1). Only divine light and grace can restore spiritual life (Ephesians 5:14).

The Bible speaks also of a more serious separation from God which it calls 'the second death' (Revelation 21:8). This means *eternal* separation from God, being shut out from His presence for ever (see chapter 10).

5   *Because we live amongst others our sin affects other lives besides our own*

Material and spiritual harm may come to many because of the selfishness of a few. Those who are interested only in themselves cannot truly help other people.

6   *Unless sin is dealt with the sinner will come more and more under its power*

More sinning causes further separation from God. Instead of leading to repentance, being aware of God's condemnation can lead to more open rebellion against His will.

7   *The truth about sin is realized most of all when it is seen in contrast with the perfect goodness of God*

(a)   *The worst thing about sin is that it fights against God.*
       This is clearly seen:
       (i)   *When men are challenged by the person of Jesus.*
             Their evil nature fights against His goodness (John 15:22-25).
       (ii) *When the Holy Spirit meets with the spirit of evil in human lives* (Galatians 5:17).

(b)   *This truth makes two things clear about salvation:*
       (i)   *The kind of remedy it brings.*
             Salvation deals with the cause, not just the effects of sin.
       (ii) *The power needed to bring this about.*
             We do not have the power or the will to save ourselves. Only the saving power of God, through the Holy Spirit, can give victory over sin.

8   *We cannot fully understand sin and why it exists*

Salvation, however, does not depend on full understanding but on full trust in the divine power which brings freedom from sin (Romans 6:19-23).

Though we cannot explain everything about sin, we know the truth that 'where sin abounded, grace did much more abound' (Romans 5:20).

Section VII. The different ways of sinning

1   *The law of God is meant to rule our inward as well as our outward life*

Thus the Bible speaks of sin in *action, motive, feeling* and *desire*.

- *(a)* *Sinful actions.* God has said 'Thou shalt' as well as 'Thou shalt not'. So God's law can be disobeyed in two ways:
    - (i) *by doing that which God forbids;* and
    - (ii) *by not doing that which He commands.*
- *(b)* *Sinful motives.* This has to do with the *reason* we do something or do not do it. Good things should be done for the right reasons and by the right power.
- *(c)* *Sinful feelings,* such as hatred, pride and greed are also condemned. God's law requires that nobler feelings—especially love—shall move us to action.
- *(d)* *Sinful desires.* God's law calls for mankind to desire only what is good and to reject what is evil. Thus, in speaking of sinful desires, the Bible deplores the absence of good intentions (Isaiah 42:24) and condemns those that are evil (2 Kings 17:17).
- *(e)* It is necessary to understand that sin is:
    - (i) not being or not doing what we know God requires, or

54

(ii) being or doing what we know God forbids. The whole person—action, motive, feeling and desire—is involved in this.

2   *Sins of motive or desire call for greater concern than sinful actions*

Wrong motive and desire are the hidden evils of heart and will which are sinful of themselves (Matthew 5:22, 28) and which lead to sinful actions.

God sees the motive behind all human actions (1 Samuel 16:7). For this reason some acts condemned by men are not condemned by God (see Mark 14:4-9), while other acts which please men do not please God (Matthew 6:1-18).

3   *Guilt is greater or less according to the light and understanding received, and to how much the whole person is involved in the wrongdoing*

Thus Jesus said to Pilate: 'The deeper guilt lies with the man who handed me over to you' (John 19:11, *New English Bible*).

There are:

(a) *Sins of weakness, when there is no desire or intention to sin* (Romans 7:19, 20).

(b) *Times when sudden and unexpected temptation causes failure.*

(c) *Sins that result from doing wrong along with others.* The innocent are sometimes led by evil-minded people into sinning (Romans 1:29-32).

(d) *Sins that are purposely intended* (Ecclesiastes 8:11) *or are the outcome of evil living.*

(e) *Sins of wilful rebellion against God* when the sinner is proud of his sins and does not regret them (Psalm 2:2, 3).

4   *The light of the gospel brings a challenge not only to man's sinful actions, but also to his sinful condition*

The gospel offers the cure for both the cause and the results of his sin. He who rejects the gospel makes his sinful state his own by choice. He is condemned both for his sins and for refusing to be saved from them (John 3:19).

Section VIII. The sinner and the wrath of God

1   *All men must face God's wrath or judgment for the sin which He hates* (see Psalm 5:4-6 and Ephesians 2:3)

2   *Bible statements about the wrath of God should be read in the light of His love for us and for righteousness* (Psalm 11:5-7)

Though the sinner must face God's judgment, he is also the object of God's love. His love is a holy love which is completely against sin. God's love is shown in His seeking to separate man from his sin and to lead him also to hate it.

3   *God is very patient with sinners*

Although the sinner must face God's judgment (Romans 2:5), God acts with grace and patience towards him.

(a) *The Bible has much to say about God's gracious dealings with the sinner* (eg, Psalm 103:8, 10; 130:3, 4; Isaiah 48:9).

(b) *God's patience can be abused* (Romans 2:4) *or misunderstood.*
The fact that God is gracious and patient with sinners does not mean that He is weak or careless

about sin, or that the day of judgment will not come (Romans 2:2, 3). The Bible says that God is not slow to keep His promise, as some men think, 'but that He is very patient . . . because it is not His will for any to be lost, but for all to come to repentance' (2 Peter 3:9, *New English Bible*).

4   *The sinner justly faces the wrath of God because of the sin for which he alone is to be blamed*

He must answer for his own wrongdoing, also for the harm this may have caused to others. He will not be blamed for the sins of others.

The suffering which comes to some people because of the sins of others is not God showing His wrath. God's wrath is against those who cause the suffering (Matthew 18:7).

6

Salvation provided

'We believe that the Lord Jesus Christ has by His suffering and death made an atonement for the whole world so that whosoever will may be saved' (Article 6).

Section I. Introduction

1 *This Article states three main truths:*
  (a) *Jesus died to make an 'atonement' for the world's sin* (see paragraph 2).
  (b) *His atoning death makes salvation possible for all mankind.*
  (c) *Each person must be willing to be saved.*
In this chapter we are thinking about how Jesus made salvation possible. What it means to be saved is dealt with in the next three chapters.

2 *There is a wide range of teaching about our belief in Christ as Saviour*
Certain words are used in trying to explain this doctrine but no single word can contain the whole truth.
  In Article 6 the word 'atonement' is used to describe what Jesus did to make salvation possible. However, the real meaning of the word 'atonement' is that the sinner is made 'at one' with God, which is part of the truth about salvation.

The word 'redemption' is used in this chapter to describe the total saving work of God in Christ, even though this word also has a limited meaning (see section III).

3   *Redemption is God's greatest work*

  (a) It is divine work—beyond human thought and power. Unlike God's other works which He brought into effect by His spoken word (Psalm 33:9), in order to bring redemption it was necessary for God in Christ to face human suffering, sin and death.

  (b) It is therefore a work unlike any other. It stands alone and was done once for all time.

  (c) Because it is a great work it brings great blessings. It makes possible a right relationship between man and God, which would be impossible by other means.

  (d) It is a matter of greatest importance to all mankind. To make this truth known is the Bible's main purpose and the chief duty of every believer.

4   *Man depends on God, not only for redemption, but also for his knowledge of it*

The Christian gospel gives equal importance to:

  (a) the death of Jesus as a fact of history, and

  (b) the eternal meaning of this happening for men.

  Both Old and New Testaments have a part in this revelation.

5   *Teaching about God's work of redemption must be linked with all other divine truth*

This will save us from accepting one part of the truth as the whole truth.

(a) Although it was Jesus who died for the sins of the world, it should be remembered that the Father, Son and Holy Spirit are involved in every divine work. In 2 Corinthians 5:19 we read that 'God was in Christ, reconciling the world unto Himself . . .'. Redemption therefore is the work of *God* and the work of *Christ.*

(b) The 'suffering and death' of Jesus should be seen as part of His complete mission. The Incarnation, Crucifixion, Resurrection and Ascension are necessary to each other and all are part of the divine work of redemption (see 1 Timothy 1:15; Hebrews 2:17; Romans 4:25; Hebrews 9:24; 7:25).

(c) The 'suffering' unto death of Jesus means more than *physical* suffering. His suffering in mind and spirit cannot be fully understood but we see something of it by His inner experience in Gethsemane (Matthew 26:37, 38; Luke 22:44) and on other such occasions (eg, John 12:27; Mark 15:34).

(d) We use the past tense in saying that Jesus *has made* an atonement for sin. This points to the fact of His complete victory and finished work at Calvary (see John 19:30; Romans 6:10; Hebrews 10:12).

This 'finished work' of Christ is a work done *for* us in order that the saving work might be done *in* us. Jesus has prepared the way whereby we can receive further blessings (John 7:39; Acts 2:33; Ephesians 4:8) and for the final setting up of the Kingdom (Acts 3:21; 1 Corinthians 15:24, 25).

(e) The atoning work of Jesus can benefit only those

who come to know Jesus Himself. Just to believe a doctrine is not enough. Salvation comes through Him who suffered and died and lives for ever to save. For all people He is both the *way* to the Father and the *means* by which God's saving grace can come to them (1 John 5:12).

(f) Jesus died for the sins of 'the whole world' (1 John 2:2), which means the human race. The New Testament speaks of His atoning work having an even wider effect (see Ephesians 1:9, 10; Colossians 1:19, 20).

(g) Finally, the work of redemption is not the only purpose served by the self-giving of Jesus. By His suffering and death:

   (i) He completes His revelation of God's great love (1 John 3:16).

  (ii) He draws forth the love and trust of those for whom He died (1 John 4:19).

 (iii) He becomes Lord over all people and all things (Romans 14:9; Philippians 2:9, 10).

Section II. The atoning death of Jesus

1 *The death of Jesus at the hands of men was a necessary part of His mission*

(a) *Salvation through Christ was in God's eternal plan* (1 Peter 1:18-20).

(b) *This being so, His death was foretold* (Acts 3:18; 1 Corinthians 15:3).

(c) *Although in one sense the Crucifixion was the work of men, they were able to act only because it was in God's plan and He allowed it* (Acts 2:23; see paragraph 2(f)).

(d) *The Crucifixion also depended on the willing obedience of Jesus.*

God gave His Son (John 3:16; Romans 8:32) but Jesus gave Himself in obedience (Philippians 2:8; John 10:11, 17, 18).

(e) *The death of Jesus was followed by His Resurrection and Ascension, and by the coming of the Holy Spirit at Pentecost* (Acts 2:1-4).

This is proof that His saving work was completed and accepted by God the Father (Romans 6:10; Acts 2:32-36).

2   *Jesus died as the Saviour of mankind*

(a) *Calvary had a very different meaning for Jesus compared with what it meant for most of those who saw Him die.*

His enemies saw Him as a religious rebel and a trouble-maker whose influence would end with His death.

To Jesus His death was the means by which His mission would be carried out (John 12:24).

(b) *The eternal view and meaning of Calvary is shown in the Bible.* (See 1 John 3:16; 1 Peter 3:18; 2:24; Matthew 26:28).

Christ died for the sinner (Romans 5:6), offering one sacrifice for sins for ever (Hebrews 10:12). The sinless One bore the guilt of sinners (2 Corinthians 5:21, *New English Bible*) and became 'an accursed thing' to free men from the curse of breaking God's law (Galatians 3:13, *New English Bible*).

(c) *The death of Jesus completed His work as the Son of man.*

As a man He had shared human experience. He

accepted the Cross for our sake, giving Himself to carry away our sins.

(d) *The death of Jesus also completed His mission on earth as the incarnate Son of God* (Philippians 2:8).

In His death He spoke for *men to the Father* even as, during His life on earth, He spoke for *God to men.* Thus He fully made known God's love for us—a love that has never changed. The sacrifice made by His Son was not the cause but the result of God's love for the sinner. This was God showing that He has always loved us (John 3:16; 1 John 4:9, 10; Romans 3:25; 2 Corinthians 5:19).

(e) *Jesus gave Himself as both Son of God and Son of man, a truth which is the heart of the gospel.*

He still gives Himself as Son of God (Galatians 2:20) and Son of man (John 3:14). He is the Way by which the sinner can be restored to God's favour and through Him the blessings of salvation come to mankind.

(f) *The Crucifixion is seen also as an act of man. Not only did Jesus die for mankind, but He died at the hands of men.*

This shows how the human heart tends to reject the spiritual light which reveals sin. Men were free to reject Jesus and they did so because they desired the darkness more than light (John 3:19).

Men have always behaved this way (Matthew 5:10-12; Acts 7:51, 52). Those who brought Jesus to His death were not sinners above all others, but mainly were responsible leaders who could not admit that they were wrong. Thus while the Cross shows God's love and desire to save mankind, it also shows how men turn against the message and

Lordship of Christ. Each one must decide for himself what the Cross is to mean to him.

3 *The Cross is the place of victory as well as of suffering*

(a) *At Calvary Jesus faced the final challenge in His fight against evil.*
He had always spoken against evil during His life on earth and successfully defended Himself against its attacks (Hebrews 4:15; John 14:30). As Son of man He now faced this final challenge in the strength of holy love. We must see Him therefore not only as One who suffered because of evil, but also as the One who challenged its power victoriously.

(b) *The New Testament shows the Cross as the place where evil was finally defeated.*
Christ took upon Himself the burden of human sin and carried it away for ever. His resurrection was the proof of His final victory over the power of evil (Hebrews 10:12-14; Romans 6:9, 10; Colossians 2:15).

(c) *All believers can share in the victory won for them by the Son of man* (Romans 6:6; 8:3, 4; 2 Corinthians 5:14, 15).

(d) *Christ conquered the power of evil which seemed to be conquering Him.*
He trusted Himself to the Father and, by His victory,

    (i) showed that evil cannot harm those who do not yield to its power;

    (ii) showed how the power of divine love conquers the worst that the enmity of sinful man can do; and

64

(iii) changed the Cross from a sign of shame into the sign of man's salvation.

Section III. The nature of salvation

1 *The meaning of special words used to describe God's saving work*

(a) 'Atonement' (being made one) and 'reconciliation' both mean the bringing together as friends those who had been against one another (see Romans 5:10, 11).

(b) 'Redeem', 'redemption' and 'ransom' all speak of someone who is bound and helpless, as a prisoner, being set free (Ephesians 1:7; Revelation 5:9). References to Christ being a ransom (Matthew 20:28; Mark 10:45) remind us that the sinner was made free by God alone at great cost (1 Peter 1:18, 19). (See also 1 Corinthians 6:19, 20.)

(c) 'Propitiation' is the English translation of a Greek word meaning forgiveness for those justly facing God's wrath (see Romans 3:25; 1 John 2:2; 4:10).

(d) The use of these words shows that Jesus saves from the *separation*, the *slavery* and the *condemnation* which sin brings.
By using different words salvation is likened to the finding of the lost, buying freedom for a slave, making an enemy into a friend, the freeing of a prisoner, the pardon of the guilty, a raising from the dead and being adopted into God's family and Kingdom.

(e) Such phrases, including 'cleansing through Christ's Blood' and 'life through His death', point

65

to the Cross as the means by which these blessings come.

The gospel also speaks of Jesus as the Saviour, the Lamb of God, the Good Shepherd, the Way to God, our High Priest, Advocate (or Mediator) and Ransom. No single word or phrase can say exactly what Christ has done for us. Therefore all should be used with care and in keeping with the whole passage or doctrine we are studying.

2 *Bible teaching about the wide purpose of redemption*

Jesus died in order that:

(i) *Sinners can be forgiven for His sake* (Ephesians 1:7; 4:32; Colossians 1:14; 1 John 2:12).

(ii) *Man can be separated from his sin* (Galatians 1:4; Hebrews 9:26; 1 John 3:5).

(iii) *The work and power of Satan can be destroyed* (Hebrews 2:14; 1 John 3:8).

(iv) *Man can be drawn to his Saviour and so restored to God's favour* (John 12:32; 2 Corinthians 5:19).

(v) *Man can share in divine life* (John 3:16; Galatians 4:5; 1 Peter 2:24).

(vi) *Man can accept His Lordship and His example of life* (2 Corinthians 5:15; 1 Peter 2:21; Philippians 2:5).

(vii) *Believers can share in a new spiritual fellowship with Him and with each other* (Ephesians 2:13-16; 5:25-27; 1 Peter 2:9, 10).

The greatest purpose of redemption is to make sinful men more and more like Jesus by the Holy Spirit's power.

3   *New Testament references to the Blood of Christ*

Almost all references in the New Testament to the Blood of Christ point to the saving power released by His death. The Jews were taught to give special respect to blood because, to them, it represented life (see Leviticus 17:11, 12).

In keeping with this Old Testament way of thinking, the Blood of Jesus represents for us His life in its total value. Being 'saved by the Blood' means being saved by the power of the life, death and rising again of the Lord Jesus Christ.

With His Blood (the value and power of His victorious life, death and resurrection) He enters the human heart (see John 6:53-57).

Section IV. Explaining the work of redemption

1   *What did the death of Jesus accomplish?*

The following answers have been given to this question, but none gives more than a part of the whole truth (see also section III, paragraph 2).

- *(a)* *His death was a ransom.* This speaks of Calvary as being the price Jesus paid to free man from a debt or obligation he cannot meet himself.

- *(b)* *His death satisfied the needs of God's law.* It was a sacrifice of such great value that God is able to let His love and mercy flow in forgiveness to those who repent for their sins and trust the Saviour.

   At the same time God's justice is upheld and the terrible evil of sin made known.

- *(c)* *His death was the victory over evil which frees man from its slavery.*

(d) His death appeals to man's conscience and heart, convincing him of God's love and leading him to repentance.

2 *Such explanations are helpful but are not essential to salvation*

To know that Christ is Saviour, and that He is the full and final revelation of God's nature and will, is greater than any explanation of the fact.

All who believe may experience salvation, even though they will never be able fully to explain it (1 Timothy 3:16; Romans 11:33, 34; John 3:8). Their trust is in Jesus—in what God has done and is now doing through Him.

Section V. The extent of God's saving purpose

1 *God's saving purpose is for everyone—the whole world*

The Bible teaches that:

(a) It is God's will that all should be saved (1 Timothy 2:4; 2 Peter 3:9; 1 John 4:14).

(b) In carrying out God's will Christ became the Saviour of all mankind.

    (i) The Bible shows that His saving work was for all the world (John 1:29; 12:32; 2 Corinthians 5:15; 1 Timothy 2:6; Hebrews 2:9).

    (ii) Therefore He can save us from all the sinful results of man's fall (Romans 5:18; 1 John 3:8; Isaiah 53:6; Titus 2:11).

    (iii) Christ Himself offered the blessings of salvation to all mankind (Matthew 11:28; John 7:37; Revelation 3:20; 21:6).

(c) *The blessings of salvation are offered freely and equally to all mankind* (Luke 2:10, 11; John 3:16; Acts 10:43; 1 Timothy 4:10).
Thus an Old Testament promise was fulfilled (see Joel 2:32; Acts 2:5, 16-21).

(d) *The Lord Jesus Christ gives to His followers the duty of carrying the gospel to all mankind* (Luke 24:46, 47; Matthew 28:19; Acts 1:8 etc).
In this they are co-workers with the Holy Spirit (John 16:8).

(e) *Though Christ died for everyone, any who refuse salvation will be eternally lost* (see 2 Peter 2:1; Hebrews 10:29; 2 Thessalonians 2:10).
They are lost not because they *could* not, but because they *would* not be saved (John 5:40; Matthew 23:37).

2 *Where the Bible says plainly that all mankind may be saved, there are those who teach that salvation is for 'the elect' only*

(a) This teaching says that the fate of each person is decided before he is born. It is claimed that God has chosen who shall and who shall not be saved, that His decision cannot be changed, and that this will be confirmed at the Last Judgment. It is also claimed that God's 'elect' can never lose their salvation.

(b) This idea that it is God's will for some to be saved and everyone else to be lost is not in keeping with His nature made known in Christ. It is therefore not the true gospel we are called to preach (Mark 16:15, 16 etc).

3 *Such teaching is wrongly based on certain Bible*

verses about God's foreknowledge and control of all things

(a) The fact that God knows beforehand how we will use our gift of choice to accept salvation, does not take away our free will or our responsibility for our decisions (see Matthew 23:36-39).

(b) Neither does God's control over all things affect our freedom of choice. Our character is formed by the choices we make. God has decided that those whose *character* makes them fit to do so may enjoy the blessings they deserve. It is character that counts, whoever the person may be.

(c) In His dealings with mankind God chose certain persons for special work, eg Jeremiah (1:5), Saul (Acts 9:15), and chose Israel to be His special people (Deuteronomy 7:6). Such 'election' was never to eternal safety but to duty. They were chosen only because God had a work for them to do. If they failed, they lost their privilege (Revelation 2:5).

Section VI. The need for man to respond to the offer of salvation

1 *The truth that Christ died for all mankind does not mean, necessarily, that all men will be saved*

Because we have freedom of choice no one can be saved against his will. We can accept or reject God's saving purpose for our life.

The Bible shows that our response to Christ's offer is the most important choice we can make—a choice between life and death.

2 *Only those who become one with Christ can receive the full benefits of His sacrifice*

God wills that we should be born again by His Spirit in whose power we can live as His children. The saving work of Christ has to do with God's whole purpose for ourselves—with what He does *for* us and what He can do *in* us.

Christ's victory over evil does not set His followers free from temptation. But He who won the victory *for* us can live victoriously *within* us (see John 16:33; 17:15; Romans 8:36, 37; Ephesians 6:10-12).

Section VII. The need to make the gospel known

1 *The gospel must be made known*

It is the preaching of the gospel that leads people to believe in Christ (Romans 10:12, 14, 17).

2 *The Holy Spirit makes believers able for this task*

   (a) *The Spirit uses those who are saved to lead and help others* (2 Corinthians 5:18-20).

   By this means the world has been given:

   (i) the Bible,

   (ii) many other writings about the Christian gospel,

   (iii) the blessings of Christian service and witness.

   (b) Every Christian is called to this duty and should:

   (i) work with faith that everyone can be saved (1 Timothy 2:1-6; Matthew 9:36-38);

   (ii) support every means possible to spread the gospel;

   (iii) give personal witness for Christ.

3   *Many have never heard of the gospel*

  (a) Such people are not guilty of unbelief as are those who have heard the gospel and refused it.

  (b) The fact that some do not know the way of salvation is not a sign that God does not care for them.

  He is still their Creator, Preserver and Governor and His love and grace reach out to them (see Acts 17:25, 27; 10:34, 35).

  (c) None is without some measure of light (Romans 1:20).

  (d) All must answer to God for their response to the light they have been shown.

  Those who have not heard the gospel will be judged by 'the law written in their hearts' (Romans 2:15). (See also Romans 2:6, 11, 12.)

  This same rule applies to everyone. Those who have received most light have the greatest responsibility (Luke 12:48; see also Matthew 11:20-24; 12:41, 42).

  (e) The continual need to spread the gospel is a challenge to all believers.

  All people need the gospel and have a right to hear it. It is our duty to take it to them (1 Corinthians 9:16).

7

Receiving salvation

'We believe that repentance towards God,
faith in our Lord Jesus Christ, and
regeneration by the Holy Spirit, are necessary
to salvation' (Article 7).
'We believe that we are justified by grace
through faith in our Lord Jesus Christ and
that he that believeth hath the witness in
himself' (Article 8).

Section I. Introduction

1 *Articles 7, 8, 9 and 10 are all about salvation as a
personal experience*
  (a) These Articles together explain the truth in Article
      6 that 'whosoever *will* may be *saved'*.
      They speak of:
        (i) *the way to receive salvation* (see sections I to
            III);
       (ii) *the blessings of salvation* (see sections IV to
            VII) and how spiritual growth leads to holy
            living.
  (b) Along with Article 11 they show how the ex-
      perience of salvation grows with time. There is:
        (i) *a first experience* (Articles 7 and 8)—that of
            conversion (Ephesians 1:12, 13);

(ii) *an on-going experience* (Articles 9 and 10)—the new life continued and developed (2 Peter 3:18); and

(iii) *a final experience* (Article 11)—salvation's full purpose reached (1 John 3:2).

(c) We are thinking about Articles 7 and 8 together in this chapter because they are both about receiving salvation and the blessings of this experience.

2   *Repentance toward God and faith in our Lord Jesus Christ are necessary to salvation* (Acts 20:21).

(a) The seeker repents and, at the same time, believes that he will be accepted by God.

(b) It is important to remember that it is God's light and love which lead the seeker to repent and believe. God's grace is *seeking* as well as *saving* grace.

(c) But man can refuse to respond to God's grace. God will neither force him to repent nor repent for him. Repentance and faith depend on God and man acting together.

Section II. Repentance towards God

1   *Repentance means a sincere decision to turn away from sin and obey God*

The word 'repentance' means to change one's mind or to turn from one thing to another. Thus the sinner turns away from sin by God's help. He is sorry before God for his sin with 'godly sorrow' (see 2 Corinthians 7:10).

2   *True repentance includes:*

(a) Conviction of sin—knowing that one is guilty of

74

doing wrong and deserves punishment (Psalm 51:4; see also Genesis 42:21; Psalm 38:4).

(b) *Hatred of sin*—turning against sin, knowing how God hates evil.

(c) *Sorrow for sin*—feeling ashamed of the sinful life that has grieved a loving God (see Psalm 38:18; Matthew 26:75).

(d) *Giving up sin.* True repentance means that the sinner has decided to finish with wrongdoing (Isaiah 55:7). Power to do this comes with salvation.

(e) *Confession of sin.* The penitent confesses his sins before God and is willing to confess them before others, especially those against whom he has sinned (Proverbs 28:13; Luke 15:21).

(f) *Desire for forgiveness* (Psalm 51:1; Luke 18:13). It is this that moves the sinner to repentance.

(g) *Surrender to God*—being willing to please Him in all things (2 Chronicles 30:8; Acts 9:6).

(h) *Willingness to make amends*—to put right, as far as one can, any wrong that has been done (Luke 19:8; see also Numbers 5:7).

As a wise father will not forgive a child for disobedience until that child has shown he is sorry and is willing to obey, so God looks for true repentance before He can forgive the sinner.

We should not depend on feelings. Feelings may differ from one person to another. There may be feelings of deep sorrow or of great relief, or mixed feelings or no feelings at all. Repentance goes beyond feelings but calls for decision and action.

Section III. Faith in our Lord Jesus Christ

1 *Saving faith is an act of trust by which the sinner enters the experience of 'being saved'*
  (a) Faith, in everyday life, is trusting or relying on someone or something we feel we can trust.
  (b) Faith is all-important when we come to God (Hebrews 11:6). Salvation can be received only by believing God's promise.
  (c) 'Saving faith' is the act of trusting and giving ourselves to God, accepting His free salvation.

2 *More about saving faith*
  (a) It is a *personal* faith.
      Each person must receive the gospel for himself— 'Who loved *me* and gave himself for *me*' (Galatians 2:20).
  (b) It is faith that *depends only on God.* The seeker no longer relies on anyone or anything else.
      Whoever wants to be saved must believe in the grace of God made known in Jesus, not in any of his own good deeds (Titus 3:4-6).
  (c) It *comes alive in response to the gospel message* (Romans 10:17; Ephesians 1:13).
  (d) It must be *accompanied by repentance* (see section 1, paragraph 2).
  (e) It leads to *the giving of one's life to God.*
      Saving faith is more than believing with the mind (see James 2:14-20). It is also an acting faith as when the believer says, 'I am trusting You *now* with my whole life.'

3 *Faith is shown in both resting on God's promises and doing God's will*

76

The believer:

(a) relies on God with *inward trust* that 'worketh not, but believeth . . .' (Romans 4:5);

(b) in *believing prayer* waits for God to keep His promises (Psalm 27:14; 2 Corinthians 1:20);

(c) goes forward in *trusting obedience* and dedication to do God's will.

4 *Helpful examples of repentance and faith are found*

(a) *in the Psalms of penitence* (especially 32, 38, 51 and 130) and

(b) *in Paul's experience*—turning from unbelief (Acts 9:1-20; 22:6-16) and from self-righteousness (Philippians 3:7-12).

Section IV. Blessings of salvation—justification

1 *We are justified by grace through faith in our Lord Jesus Christ*

(a) To be 'justified' means to be declared 'just' or 'right' before the law. In the Bible the word 'justification' has a close link with the word 'righteousness' (see Romans 3:21, 22, 24; Philippians 3:9).

(b) The Bible speaks of two ways in which men seek to be justified before God (see Acts 13:38, 39; Galatians 2:16):

(i) By the working of the law (legal justification). *Legal justification is for the innocent* who is declared to be 'just' because he is proved innocent (Deuteronomy 25:1).

(ii) By faith in Jesus (Christian justification). *Christian justification is for the guilty* who is declared to be 'just' because of his repentance and faith in Christ (Romans 4:5).

These two are quite different in God's sight. To claim one means giving up any claim to the other (see Galatians 2:21 and 5:4).

Justification by grace through faith in Christ is the only way we can be saved. We cannot justify ourselves (Galatians 3:22).

2 *Justification is seen as God being both merciful and just*

(a) *His mercy* is seen in His gracious gift of Jesus to be our atoning Saviour (1 John 4:10).

(b) *His justice* is seen when He justifies those who come to Him with faith in Christ's atoning work (see 1 John 1:9).

3 *Those who are justified know that they are sinners saved by grace*

No one can separate himself from the rest of mankind. We who receive mercy must show mercy to others. Our new relationship with God will change our relationship with people (Matthew 5:7; 6:12, 14, 15; 18:21-35; Luke 17:3, 4; Ephesians 4:32; Colossians 3:13; James 2:12, 13).

4 *Justification brings to us restored fellowship with God*

Therefore:

(a) we are freed from condemnation (Romans 8:1);

(b) we enjoy God's favour (Romans 5:1); and

(c) we are kept humble in knowing the cost of our pardon (1 Peter 2:24).

5 *However, the results of past sins cannot be wholly undone*

  (a) Earthly blessings—health, reputation, friendships—lost by sinning are not always restored, though they may, in part, be regained by right living.

  (b) The effects of sinning upon the lives of others may remain, but much can be done, by God's help, to heal these effects.

Section V. Blessings of salvation—regeneration by the Holy Spirit

1 *'Regeneration' is one of the words used to describe the great change brought about by the Holy Spirit in those whose sins are forgiven*

  (a) Regeneration means 'being born again' or 'the coming of new life'.

  (b) This spiritual change has both an immediate and a following effect. We shall learn how God's salvation meets the continuing needs of the awakened sinner when we study Articles 9 and 10. In this chapter, however, we are thinking about the first change caused by the coming of new life to the soul.

2 *Words used to explain regeneration show how great is the change that is brought about*

It is described as:

  (a) *Becoming a new creature* (2 Corinthians 5:17; Galatians 6:15). This means not just an improvement, but a new creative act of God.

(b) Being born again—'born of the Spirit' (John 3:6; see also John 3:7; 1 Peter 1:23).
This means a new beginning, a new character and a new relationship with God.

(c) Passing from death to life (John 5:24; 1 John 3:14).

(d) Passing from darkness to light (John 8:12; Ephesians 5:8; 1 Thessalonians 5:5).

(e) Receiving eternal life (John 17:2; Romans 6:23).
Here eternal life means life which has the nature and qualities of the life that is to come. It is knowing God and living in fellowship with Him through Jesus the Son (John 17:3; 1 John 5:20).

(f) Becoming the temple of the indwelling Spirit (1 Corinthians 6:19).

3   *The greatness of this change is seen in the way it happens*

(a) It is brought about by the Holy Spirit working in the power of the risen Christ (compare John 7:39 with Acts 2:32, 33).

(b) The Spirit works together with the Father and the Son. Thus we read also of God the Father and of Christ living and working in the hearts of believers (see Philippians 2:13; Colossians 1:27; Ephesians 3:16, 17).

4   *This new beginning should lead to the bringing about of God's eternal purpose* (Philippians 1:6).

God's purpose is to draw us into fellowship with Himself so that we may become like Him (Genesis 1:26; 1 John 3:2).

5 *Our human minds cannot fully understand the work of regeneration*

Yet we know that it is true when we experience this change for ourselves (see John 3:8; Ephesians 3:20).

Section VI. Blessings of salvation—adoption into God's family

Adoption is God receiving into His family the forgiven and 'born again' sinner.

1 *This act of grace brings us into a relationship with God as Father that we do not have by natural birth*

- *(a)* All people are God's children, for He is their Creator (Acts 17:24-29). But only those who are saved through Jesus Christ have the right to be called *sons* or *children* of God in a spiritual sense (John 1:12, 13).
- *(b)* When we receive Jesus as Saviour, God's eternal purpose, that we should be His children, is made real in each life (Galatians 3:26; 4:4, 5, 7; Ephesians 1:4, 5).
- *(c)* Those who become children of God also become citizens of His Kingdom (Ephesians 2:19).

2 *Adoption leads to spiritual union with all other children of God*

This union in Christ binds His followers to one another in a close and lasting relationship (Galatians 3:28; Romans 12:3-5; 1 Corinthians 12:12-20; Ephesians 2:16-22; 4:1-16; 1 Peter 2:4-10).

3   *Adoption brings great spiritual blessings*

   (a) The Bible speaks of blessings 'according to God's grace' and 'according to His glory', of being 'heirs of God and joint-heirs with Christ' (Romans 8:17) and of receiving all blessings in and with Him (Romans 8:32; Ephesians 1:3).

   (b) The Bible tells of the wealth of these spiritual blessings which are also made known by the Holy Spirit (1 Corinthians 2:9, 10; Ephesians 1:15-18).

   (c) The Bible shows that adoption brings men into a special relationship with:

      (i) *The Father* (John 20:17) from whom comes 'every good and perfect gift' (James 1:17). His loving care exceeds that of the best human parents (Luke 11:13).

     (ii) *The Son* who shares with us His glory (John 12:26; 14:3; Romans 8:17; Ephesians 1:11; Hebrews 2:11) and the loving relationship that He has with the Father (John 17:24, 26; 15:9).

    (iii) *The Holy Spirit,* who works in the life with the same power that raised Christ from the dead to His throne of glory (Romans 8:11; Ephesians 1:19-23).

   (d) God has not yet made known all the blessings He has planned for His children. By faith we receive present blessings and believe we shall receive those which are to come (Romans 8:18-25).

Section VII. Blessings of salvation—assurance

Assurance of salvation means knowing without doubt that we are forgiven and accepted by God. This assurance is given by the Holy Spirit and is proved by experience.

1 *The Holy Spirit gives this inward assurance in two ways*

 (a) He causes us to know Christ as a present and personal Saviour.

 Article 8 makes it clear that when we are saved we know it. This truth is found in 1 John 5:10. We read in the same epistle that the Spirit of Truth brings this inward knowledge of Jesus as personal Saviour. This knowledge makes us confident to claim all the spiritual blessings Jesus gives (Hebrews 4:16; 10:19-22).

 (b) He makes us sure of our adoption (Romans 8:15; Galatians 4:6).

2 *This inward witness of the Spirit is proved by the outward witness of a changed life*

This is the main theme of the First Epistle of John. The words 'we know' appear again and again, showing how we may be sure that we are born again as children of God, that we have passed from death to life, and that God dwells in us and we in Him.

 The divine nature will be seen in the life of the child of God.

3 *Assurance is further proved by Christian progress*

 (a) Growth in grace brings 'the full assurance of understanding' (Colossians 2:2).

 (b) Knowing God's guidance makes us sure that He is in control of our life (2 Corinthians 1:10).

 (c) Spiritual fruit (Galatians 5:22) will be the sign of the Spirit's continuing power and influence in our life (John 15:1, 2, 5).

8

Keeping salvation

'We believe that continuance in a state of salvation depends upon continued obedient faith in Christ' (Article 9).

Section I. Introduction

This Article, with Article 10, deals with the Christian life after conversion.

The heart of this teaching is that the Christian must continue to depend on Christ as Saviour and Lord, living a life of faith and obedience (John 15:4; Galatians 5:25; 2 Peter 3:18). Failure to do this results in backsliding (see section III).

Section II. Continuing to trust and obey (obedient faith)

1 *This continuing trust is the exercise of the same saving faith which brings salvation* (see chapter 7, section III)

Thus the saved person depends on God for promised help and to keep him saved.

(a) *It is faith that relies on God's grace and faithfulness* (1 Peter 5:7; 1 Corinthians 10:13; Hebrews 13:5, 6; Jude 24, 25).

(b) It is faith that continues to depend on Christ (1 John 5:11, 12).

(c) It is faith that leads to obedience to God's will and His law—one of the purposes of Christ's death (Romans 8:3, 4; 1 John 5:2, 3).

(d) It is faith that works with God in order to bring about His known purposes (1 John 3:2, 3; Philippians 3:12-14; Hebrews 12:1, 2).

(e) It is faith that dares to go forward, still trusting God to do what He has promised, especially when He calls to special service. For example, Acts 10:28, 29; 13:2, 3; Philippians 4:13.

(f) It is a growing faith, strengthened by exercise as God's faithfulness is proved.

2 *Obedience is always necessary to keep salvation*

   (a) The new life in Christ is a life of obedience.

   (i) God's children pray and offer themselves to God so that His will may be done on earth (Matthew 6:9, 10).

   (ii) They receive power to obey through the risen Saviour (Romans 8:3, 4).

   (iii) They have received the blessing of a new heart which desires to do God's will (Jeremiah 31:33; Ezekiel 36:26, 27).

   (iv) Christian obedience works by love (John 14:15; 1 John 5:3).

   (v) All who have the Spirit of Christ seek to obey God's will like Christ did (John 6:38; Philippians 2:5).

   (b) The child of God is one who always follows the leading of the Holy Spirit (Romans 8:14).

(c) *Those who disobey what they know to be God's will are falling from their spiritual state by the measure of their disobedience* (Luke 6:46; Matthew 7:26, 27; Romans 2:6-11; 6:16). Salvation is only for those who obey (Hebrews 5:9; John 15:14; 1 John 2:3, 4).

3 *Thus salvation always requires action on God's part and ours*

(a) The Holy Spirit brings to the changed heart the desire and power to serve God.

(b) Obedient faith depends all the time on the work of the Holy Spirit in the heart (Philippians 2:13; Hebrews 13:20, 21).

(c) God expects us to do all that His Spirit urges us to do (Philippians 2:12, 13).

(d) God's children will always have to face a challenge to their faith in this world (John 16:33; 2 Timothy 3:12).

Meeting this challenge can become the means by which faith is made stronger and character grows (Romans 5:3-5; 1 Peter 1:6, 7; 5:8-10; James 1:2-4).

Christ is the best example of continued obedient faith, yet this He learned through 'the things which he suffered' (Hebrews 5:8, 9; see also 12:3).

4 *Christians must always work with God in order to bring about what He desires*

(a) They should understand that God wants to do a work of grace *for* them, *within* them and *through* them.

The change in their lives and their spiritual growth shows the power and grace of salvation (Matthew 5:16; Philippians 2:14, 15; 1 Peter 2:9, 12). They can spread the news of salvation (Matthew 10:32, 33; Acts 1:8) and show the Spirit of Christ in service to others (Galatians 6:10; Matthew 5:43-48; 7:12; 25:40).

(b) Believers should therefore:

    (i) *Seek to know God's will*—by prayer, Bible reading, the Spirit's guidance and the challenge of events. Obedience to what we know of God's will opens the way for further revelation.

    (ii) *Live prayerfully*—always depending on God for grace and power to *be* and *do* what He wills (2 Corinthians 4:7; 12:9, 10; Ephesians 6:18).

    (iii) *Dedicate themselves to godly living.* This means separation in thought and deed from ungodly aims and ways of life (Romans 12:2; 1 John 2:15, 16) and giving all their powers in the cause of right (Romans 6:13; see also 12:1).

    In matters of doubt the Christian is guided by principles given in such Bible verses as Romans 14 and 1 Corinthians 8; 10:24-33.

Section III. The possibility of backsliding and rejection

1 *Backsliding is a Bible word for falling away from God after having been saved*

  (a) Those who have never been truly saved cannot be said to backslide in this sense. Nevertheless some truly saved people have lost their salvation, and this danger faces every Christian.

(b) The words 'backslidden' and 'backsliding' are used to describe

   (i) a final experience when all spiritual life is lost, and

  (ii) the process by which this state is reached.
Backsliding is often *secret* at first, but later becomes *open,* being seen in the outward life.

(c) *Failure to respond to or resisting God's will is backsliding.*

(d) *This happens in the backslider's own heart and will* (Proverbs 4:23).
He begins to fall when he says 'no' where he used to say 'yes' to the voice of God.

One wrong act is not of itself backsliding. Backsliding is determined by the attitude of heart. Where wrongdoing is followed by repentance, forgiveness can be sought and found and backsliding be prevented. But if there is no repentance the result will be backsliding with more and more separation from God.

2   *The cause of failure can be either in the backslider's faith or in his obedience*

(a) *There can be loss of faith*—a ceasing to trust in Jesus as Saviour:

   (i) by relying on some other ground of faith (see Galatians 1:6) or

  (ii) by giving up all trust in the true gospel message (1 Timothy 1:19; Hebrews 3:12).

(b) *There can be a sliding back through sinful neglect as well as through sinful acts*—neglect of prayer and the Bible, failure to witness before others or to answer a call to dedication and service; through purposely sinning and continuing to sin in thought

and deed (1 Corinthians 3:16, 17 and 9:25-27) or turning away from Christ to worldly living (2 Peter 2:20-22).

3   *When is backsliding complete?*

The two main answers are:

(a) *When a believer purposely turns away from Christ.*

He will know he has backslidden when he:

(i) rejects the demands of Christian discipleship *(disobedience)* or

(ii) *rejects Christ as Saviour (unbelief)* (see Hebrews 10:29 and 6:6).

(b) *When all spiritual dealings with God have ceased.* This can happen even though one still claims to be a Christian (see Revelation 3:1). This is the backsliding in heart that is caused by continued spiritual neglect (see John 15:1-6 and Hebrews 2:1-4).

4   *The backslider who keeps on fighting against God's will loses both present and final salvation*

(a) *The Bible teaches that those who have received new life in Christ can lose it and turn from Him* (see Matthew 5:13; John 15:6; Luke 8:13; 9:62).

We read of those who 'fall from grace' or 'fall away' (Galatians 5:4; Hebrews 6:4-6) and of the judgment they must face (see also 2 Peter 2:20, 21; 1 Timothy 4:1).

The *eternal* life which God gives is a quality of life the believer has only while he abides in Christ (see 1 John 5:11, 12; Romans 8:9). Those who are kept safe are they who *hear* Christ's voice and continue to *follow* Him (John 10:27, 28).

89

(b) Final salvation is promised only to those who are faithful to the end (Colossians 1:22, 23; Hebrews 3:14; 10:38, 39; Jude 20, 21).
Jesus Himself taught this truth when on earth (Matthew 10:22; 24:13) and from Heaven (Revelation 2:10, 25).

(c) Those who are not faithful to the end will be lost.
The Bible tells of those whom God rejects (Romans 1:28; 2 Corinthians 13:5-7; 2 Timothy 3:8; Titus 1:16).

Jesus said that many will be sent away from Him at the final judgment even though they claim to have worked successfully for Him (Matthew 7:22, 23).

Paul saw this possibility. He who could give a triumphant testimony (2 Timothy 4:7, 8), also knew that he could be finally rejected (see 1 Corinthians 9:27).

5 *The Bible teaches that everyone will be judged according to the light received*

(a) History has proved the truth the prophets taught, that special privilege brings greater responsibility (see Amos 3:1, 2; Daniel 9:11, 12; Matthew 3:7-10; Acts 13:46).

(b) Jesus taught this same truth (Matthew 11:20-24; Luke 12:48).

(c) The Epistles teach believers to learn from the example of Israel and backsliders are warned of severe judgment (Romans 11:20, 21; 1 Corinthians 10:11, 12; Hebrews 2:2, 3; 4:1; 10:29; 12:25).

(d) God has no favourites when He gives grace (Acts 10:34, 35, 43; Romans 10:12), nor in giving justice (Romans 2:6, 11, 12).
He cannot allow His children to behave in such a

way that would be condemned in the case of the ungodly (see Romans 2:8, 9; Galatians 6:7, 8; Ephesians 5:3-6 etc).

6 *Backsliding harms the cause of Christ as well as the spiritual life of the backslider*

It gives the ungodly reason to despise the name and power of God (Romans 2:21-24; 1 Timothy 6:1). The backslider is a witness against Christ and His teaching.

7 *The backslider may still receive pardon and be restored*

The gospel message of grace is not changed by human failure.

(a) The message of God's unchanging grace, given to backsliding Israel, is also given to His people today (see Jeremiah 3:12-14; Hosea 14:1-4; Revelation 2:5, 16; 3:2, 3, 16, 18-20).

(b) The way back is by repentance and faith. The backslider must receive Christ again as Lord and Saviour, trusting again in Him who pardons and restores the penitent.

(c) The backslider who continues to rebel against God can only expect to face God's judgment (Hebrews 10:26, 27).

(d) The way to be safe from backsliding is to 'walk in the Spirit' (Galatians 5:16, 25).

9

Holiness (sanctification)

'We believe that it is the privilege of all believers to be wholly sanctified, and that their whole spirit and soul and body may be preserved blameless unto the coming of our Lord Jesus Christ' (Article 10).

Section I. Introduction

1 *This Article speaks about God's call to and provision for holy living*
It is linked with Paul's words in 1 Thessalonians 5:23, 24 from which we learn:

(a) that sanctification is the work of God,

(b) that sanctification is not only a privilege but an experience to which God calls all believers (see also 1 Thessalonians 4:3; 2 Thessalonians 2:13),

(c) that sanctification is a complete work which affects the whole person—spirit, soul and body—for all time.

It is God's desire that His children should be like Him in holiness and love (1 Thessalonians 3:12, 13). This is what sanctification is about.

92

Section II. The nature of sanctification

1 *To 'sanctify' means to 'make holy'*

The word 'sanctification' is used in two ways: (1) it describes the *action* or way by which we are made holy, and (2) it can mean the *result* of this action—the state of being holy.

2 *All true holiness comes from the holiness of God*

All holy things are holy only because of their relationship to Him (see chapter 2, section II, 4*(a)*). Thus teaching about holiness in man must be linked with teaching about the holiness of God.

(a) *The word 'holy' was used in the earliest days to express God's greatness and power,* being high above and separate from all things (Isaiah 57:15). (See chapter 2, section II: 1 and 2.)

Thinking of God in this way made men afraid to worship Him except in a special way. Such reverence was also given to everything men thought of as belonging to God. Thus certain places, times, ceremonies, things and persons were set apart from other uses as being holy (separate) unto God, as were the Sabbath (Exodus 20:8-10), the Tabernacle and the priests (Leviticus 8).

(b) *As time passed the holiness of God was seen in His righteousness and perfection in every way* (Isaiah 5:16).

People came to understand what it means to be holy as they received more revelation. Anyone who claimed to represent God had to be pure in character and in actions, thus showing a reflection of God's nature (see Psalm 15 and 24:3-6; also chapter 2, section II: 4).

(c) As more was made known of God's holiness it was realized that no person, unchanged and un-cleansed, was worthy to stand before Him (Psalm 130:3, 4; 143:2; Job 25:4-6).

Yet the promise was also given that God would dwell 'with him who is broken and humble in spirit' (Isaiah 57:15, *New English Bible*). (See also Isaiah 1:11-20 and 6:1-8.) The gospel message is that we *can* be changed and cleansed as was Isaiah.

(d) In Jesus this experience of 'God in man' reached perfection and was made available to every believer.

Jesus is the way to God and through Him God's holy life comes to us. By Him all persons, all places and all seasons can be set apart for God and for His glory.

3   *To be sanctified means that we belong to God so that we are indwelt by Him* (see 2 Corinthians 6:16).

(a) Belonging to God means being 'set apart for' or 'separated to' God as were the Temple and the priests in Old Testament times. With this in mind we use terms such as consecration, dedication and offering oneself as a living sacrifice.

Being *separated to God* means being *separated from* everything that is against God or unlike His nature. Thus Paul pictures the Christian as a good soldier who keeps himself free from unsoldierly things (2 Timothy 2:3, 4).

The believer must be willing to be separated and cleansed from all that is sinful (2 Corinthians 6:14, 17; 1 John 1:6, 9).

(b) Indwelt by God means God living within us in

94

such a way that His holy nature is seen in our lives. With this thought we use the terms, being like God (Godliness), being filled with the Spirit, bearing the fruit of the Spirit, purity of heart and perfect love.

Teaching about sanctification must be accepted as a whole. There is that which we must do and that which only God can do. Sanctification calls for man's consecration and God's indwelling which makes the heart pure and the life holy (see Titus 2:14). Every movement toward holiness must mean a movement away from all that is unholy.

The word 'Christlikeness' unites and fulfils the truths about sanctification and holiness. Christ lived a life of complete consecration in which God's holy love was seen.

4 *The use of the words 'consecration' and 'sanctification'*

(a) Difficulty sometimes arises when the words 'consecrate' and 'consecration' are used to mean 'sanctify' and 'sanctification' (see Glossary).

In The Salvation Army the word 'consecration' is used to describe man's act of giving himself (dedication), while the word 'sanctification' describes God's act in accepting as holy that which is given or consecrated.

(b) When the Bible speaks of a man sanctifying himself, that man is meeting the conditions needed for God to accept and sanctify him (see Leviticus 20:7, 8).

(c) We read of Jesus being sanctified by the Father (John 10:36) and sanctifying Himself (John 17:19). This means that Jesus dedicated Himself to the work the Father had given Him to do.

5   *The holy life of Jesus was the expression of His divine nature* (Hebrews 7:26), *while holiness in us is the result of a work of divine grace*

  (a) The life of Jesus revealed much about holy living which otherwise would not have been known.

  Jesus showed that a holy life of love can be lived in a sinful world. He proved that holy living can triumph over every temptation and the power of evil (Hebrews 4:15). He lived, died and rose again, not only to be a holy example but to make it possible for sinful people to be Christlike.

  (b) We can live holy lives only when Jesus lives within us, changing us by the power of His Spirit.

  This is the sanctifying work God does *in* and *through* us by:

    (i) *freeing* from the power of self and sin,

    (ii) *cleansing* from the spoiling effects of sin, and

    (iii) *changing* completely our lives from love of self and sin to love of God and holiness. Thus wrongdoing is replaced by Christlike living.

The heart of this experience is well expressed by the words of Paul to the Galatians (see Galatians 2:20).

Holiness in human lives is the Christlike character and conduct shown by those in whom the Spirit of Christ dwells and rules.

Section III. God's provision for sanctification

1   *The Atonement provides for our sanctification* (Hebrews 13:12)

(See also Romans 8:3,4; Ephesians 5:25-27; 1 Peter 2:21, 24; 1 John 3:5, 8.)

(a) *This means that we may be sanctified in Christ even as we are justified in Christ* (see 1 Corinthians 1:30).

Justification, regeneration, adoption and sanctification are equally part of God's gift to believers. All are blessings of the New Covenant given through Jesus (Hebrews 9:15-17).

(b) *The New Testament teaches that every believer can be sanctified, enjoying all the privileges and duties this brings* (Romans 6:6; 8:12; Colossians 3:9, 10).

(See also 1 Corinthians 1:2; 3:22, 23; 6:11; Ephesians 1:3; 2:6; Colossians 3:3; Hebrews 10:10, 12-14; 1 Peter 2:9.)

(c) *This means that God's provision for our sanctification is complete.*

Where this work of grace is lacking in a Christian's life the reason can only be his failure to fully trust and obey God.

(d) *All can be holy in and through the purpose, call and provision of God.*

Romans 6, Ephesians 4-6, Colossians 3 and 4, the First Epistle of Peter and the First Epistle of John all show that if a Christian is not enjoying the *blessings* of sanctification, he is not fully claiming what God has provided. The reason may be lack of knowledge, faith or obedience. We learn also that we must accept the *duties* of sanctification. When we commit ourselves to Christ our Saviour we give ourselves for His full purpose in salvation.

2 *It is the indwelling Spirit of God who brings about*

the great change that sanctification requires and provides

(a) *The greatest blessing men can receive through the Atonement is the indwelling of the Holy Spirit,* for through Him all other blessings of salvation come. They who have the Spirit have the Spirit of Christ and may be 'filled with all the fullness of God' (Ephesians 3:16-19). This privilege makes it our duty to respond to every influence of the Spirit.

(b) *The Holy Spirit brings the life and power that makes holiness possible, while wholehearted response to the Spirit makes holiness actual* (see Romans 8:1-17).

The Bible shows that the Holy Spirit is not only the source of all goodness (Galatians 5:22, 23) but the strong enemy of all that is evil (Galatians 5:17). Man's sinful nature ('the flesh') is the root cause of his spiritual weakness. In the sanctified life the Spirit brings purity and freedom from the power of this lower nature.

Section IV. The response God requires

1 *God's call to holiness is a call to live in constant fellowship with the risen Saviour*

(a) Believers are called to be united with Christ in His death on the Cross so that, being crucified with Him, their sinful nature may die and, united with Him in the power of His resurrection, they may live a new life (2 Corinthians 5:14, 15; Colossians 3:3).

(b) *We cannot be holy unless we are freed from sin.*
Sin not only makes us do evil things; it makes our hearts and minds evil (see Mark 7:15, 21-23).

98

God's holy purpose cannot be carried out in a life so affected. 'The temple' must be clean and separated from that which causes evil (see 1 Corinthians 3:17).

(c) Only through the Atonement can we gain this freedom.

The gospel message is that God wills and has made it possible for us to be set free from sin through the risen Saviour (Romans 6:1-11).

(d) This work of grace is powerful and affects the whole person.

It is a change, through death, to a new life which leaves behind the past with its sin, self-will and self-dependence (Philippians 3:3-11).

Everything of Paul's old life was left at the Cross so that he might 'know him, and the power of his resurrection'.

Those who know death and new life in Christ are not only freed from the rule of sin, but 'created after the likeness of God in true righteousness and holiness' (Ephesians 4:24, Revised Standard Version). United to the risen Lord, they share His higher life (Ephesians 2:4, 6; Colossians 3:1-3).

2 *God, having made known that He desires and has provided for His people's sanctification, calls for us to respond in faith and consecration*

(a) This act of faith and consecration shows our trust in God's power to sanctify and our own willingness to be sanctified.

The Bible teaches that, along with sanctifying faith, there must be:

(i) a giving of ourselves fully to God;

(ii) a living out of this consecration in every part of life.

Examples of this call to consecration are found in Romans 12:1, 2; 1 Corinthians 6:19, 20; 2 Corinthians 6:16, 17; 1 Peter 1:14, 15; 1 John 3:2,3.

(b) *Sanctifying faith, like saving faith, is an act of personal trust by which we give ourselves to God and accept as our own what God so freely offers to us.*

We kneel at the same Cross as when we sought salvation and trust in the same Atonement. The same Saviour who *justified* now *sanctifies* (1 Corinthians 6:11; see also 1 Corinthians 1:30).

(c) *Consecration is also like repentance in that there is a turning to God in humble obedience and a turning from all that is against Him (renunciation).*

In holiness the believer must 'put on' godly character and equally 'put off' all that is ungodly. In saying 'Yes' to God and righteousness he says 'No' to self and sin. Thus consecration goes along with renunciation. To the question, 'What must be renounced?' the answer is, 'All that cannot be consecrated to God'.

Duties to family, business and to our neighbours must be faithfully carried out as part of our offering to God (see 1 Corinthians 10:31; Colossians 3:17, 23).

Paul speaks of these, and of other duties to Church and nation, in Romans 12 and 13, following his call to holy consecration.

(d) *Consecration to holiness includes dedication:*

    (i) *To be God's temple or dwelling place.* This calls for a heart open to receive Him and a body that is kept pure (1 Corinthians 6:17-20).

    (ii)   *To be His servant,* no longer living for self but to please Him only (Luke 9:23, 24).

    (iii) *To holiness of character and conduct.* Holiness is both inward and outward (see 2 Corinthians 7:1; Matthew 5:16; 1 Peter 2:12).

    (iv) *To holy influence.* Because God wills that all His people should be sanctified, holy living will include concern for others and every effort possible to cause them also to believe and obey (see Ephesians 4:1-16).

  (e) *In all these requirements we should take Christ as our example* (John 13:15; Romans 15:5; 1 Peter 2:21; 1 John 4:17).

Holiness is Christlikeness. It is a call:

    (i) to have the mind of Christ (Philippians 2:1-15; 1 Peter 4:1, 2);

    (ii) to 'walk in the light, as he is in the light' (1 John 1:7);

    (iii) to be pure 'as he is pure' (1 John 3:3);

    (iv) to receive one another, 'as Christ also received us' (Romans 15:7);

    (v) to 'walk in love, as Christ also hath loved us' (Ephesians 5:2);

    (vi) to forgive as we have been forgiven through Him and by Him (Ephesians 4:32; Colossians 3:13);

    (vii) to 'walk, even as he walked' (1 John 2:6).

3   *In the experience of holiness there is a crisis and a process—that which happens at once and that which goes on happening*

First there is the dedication when we give ourselves

wholly to God. Then follows the continued action by which our dedication is worked out in every part of our life.

(a) *This continued action affects character and conduct in both a negative and a positive way* (see 2 Corinthians 7:1).

    (i) The Bible speaks of this in terms of death and life: we are dead to the old life and alive to the new life in Christ (Romans 8:13; Colossians 3:3, 5).

    (ii) There is a putting off and a putting on in the believer's experience (see Romans 13:12-14).

This does not mean that we try to cast out evil by our own hard efforts. The Christian however should have nothing to do with those things Christ has condemned (Romans 8:3) and should receive and live out the new life He gives.

(b) *To fulfil his dedication the believer must commit not only his outward conduct, but also his desires and motives to the purpose and power of the indwelling Spirit.*

It is his duty to allow the spiritual gifts and graces received from God to grow, thus to share and show the divine nature (see 2 Peter 1:2-11).

This rule applies especially to the grace of love. The Bible shows that a loving nature can come only from God Himself. Love is a spiritual gift to be sought above all others (1 Corinthians 13). As a 'fruit of the Spirit' (Galatians 5:22) love will fill our hearts through the Holy Spirit, God's gift to us (see Romans 5:5, *New English Bible*).

To love is a command to God's people. Jesus said it is the greatest commandment of all (Matthew 22:36-40) and it was His chief command to His

102

disciples (John 13:34, 35). The Epistles also stress this theme of Christian love.

We cannot obey Christ's command to be loving until we give our heart and will to receive this gift of grace, and are ready to show it in our daily living. Love is especially needed when the Christian is confronted with unChristlike attitudes and conduct (see Romans 12:17-21; 1 Corinthians 13:4-7; Ephesians 4:31, 32; Colossians 3:12-14; 1 John 3:16-18). In this way the Christian follows his Master's example.

4   *The life-changing power of love is a most important part of the experience of sanctification. This is why sanctification is sometimes called the blessing of 'perfect love'* (1 John 4:7-21).

This grace of love (see 1 Timothy 1:5) is emphasized because:

- (a) *Christian love to one's neighbour fulfils in the best possible way God's law concerning human relationships* (Galatians 5:14).
- (b) *When we act in love to God and mankind we find freedom and satisfaction within ourselves.*
- (c) *To be ruled by the love of God is the way in which we become like God in character* (Matthew 5:43-48).

  This love (born of love) is shown:

  - (i) *To God,* with desire to please and serve Him and to be like Him, trusting in His grace. It is the 'perfect love' which 'casteth out fear' (1 John 4:18).
  - (ii) *To mankind* in that all people are seen to be within the purpose and power of this love (2 Corinthians 5:14).

5   *Sanctification is also spoken of as 'full salvation' for two main reasons:*

   (a) Because it is a complete work of grace that fully meets our deepest needs (see section I, paragraph 1*(c)*; section II, paragraph 5*(b)*).

   (b) Because the sanctified life is fully given to God as Lord and Saviour, and fully responds to the sanctifying grace His Spirit gives.
   Sanctification is not a state in which there can be no further progress, but one in which, through the removal of hindrances, the way is opened for continued spiritual growth (2 Corinthians 3:18; 1 John 4:12).

6   *While sanctification can be described as full salvation it is not final salvation*

   (a) Some of the blessings of salvation will not be realized in this life, notably the redemption of the body (Romans 8:23) and the change from an earthly to a glorified state (Romans 8:11, 30).

   (b) Final salvation will, among other results, bring about the change when 'the Lord Jesus Christ . . . will change our lowly body to be like His glorious body' (Philippians 3:21, Revised Standard Version). (See also 1 Corinthians 15:53, 54.)

   (c) While we are in our earthly state we cannot be free from human limitations of mind and body. As Paul says (2 Corinthians 4:7), 'we have this treasure in earthen vessels'. This truth shows that it is wrong to think:

      (i) that because we are 'earthen vessels' we cannot have the treasure;

      (ii) that if we have the treasure we will cease to be 'earthen vessels'.

(d) Sanctification, therefore, does not bring perfect knowledge such as only God possesses. It does not make us free from the possibility of mistakes. It does, however, bring the guidance of the Holy Spirit which makes us less likely to make wrong decisions. God directs the way of all who trust in Him (James 1:5; Proverbs 3:6).

(e) Sanctification does not give freedom from bodily or mental sickness. Many holy people have known such suffering. It does, however, bring grace to enable God's people to glorify Him in their sufferings and sometimes to exercise faith for healing.

(f) Nowhere is it stated in the Bible that the body is a hindrance to sanctification. We are taught that the body, with all its appetites, powers and members, is to be sanctified to God (1 Corinthians 6:20; 2 Corinthians 4:10, 11).

    (i) Bible promises about holiness which have to do with this life can be realized in this life. Both Romans 8:11 and 2 Corinthians 4:16 make clear reference to the power of God working in and through our mortal bodies.

    (ii) Our earthly state does not prevent us from living in the Spirit and following His leadings (Romans 8:13; Galatians 5:16, 25), nor from bringing forth the fruit of love (see paragraph 4). But it does encourage us to depend on God (see 2 Corinthians 12:9).

(g) The sanctified believer will still have to face temptation during his earthly life.
Jesus, though sinless, was severely tempted. The New Testament teaches that all His followers will face temptation, but that they will receive:

(i) the *spiritual weapons* to meet it (Ephesians 6:10-18);

(ii) the *promise* of divine help in standing against it (1 Corinthians 10:13); and

(iii) the *assurance* of the good that can result from it (1 Peter 1:6, 7; James 1:12).

10

The final destiny of man

'We believe in the immortality of the soul; in
the resurrection of the body; in the general
judgment at the end of the world; in the
eternal happiness of the righteous; and in the
endless punishment of the wicked' (Article 11).

Section I. Introduction

1 *Article 11 deals with what happens after death and
at the end of time*

This is a necessary part of Christian doctrine because we
must know something of what God will finally do in
order to understand what He has done up to the present.
The Bible shows that we were created for life, not only
in this world, but also in the world to come where God's
purpose for us can be fully realized.

2 *From the Bible we may learn about life after death
and of what eternity holds for us*

We learn mostly from the teaching of Jesus and of His
apostles. Although much truth has still to be made

known, we are given enough for the guidance, encouragement and warning we need.

3 *In some ways God's final acts are already taking place*

(a) *Christians experience freedom from the bondage and condemnation of this present evil world* (Galatians 1:4) *and taste the powers of the world to come* (Hebrews 6:5).
They have an experience *now* of resurrection power and of the heavenly life (John 5:24; 11:25, 26; Ephesians 2:6; Philippians 3:20; Colossians 3:3; 2 Corinthians 4:16).

(b) *Unbelievers face God's judgment even now and know something of the separation from Him which their unbelief brings* (John 3:18, 36; 12:31).

(c) *There are things in the present that will not pass away, even at the end of time.*
These are 'those things which cannot be shaken'.
Only the things that belong to time will be removed (2 Corinthians 4:18; Hebrews 12:26-29).

4 *Bible teaching about the life to come is given for our benefit in this life*
We are told that we will face, in the life to come, the consequences of the life we now live.

The purpose of this revelation is that all may seek and know Christ as Saviour. The value of such teaching is measured by its effect in causing us to live in the light of eternity (see 2 Peter 3:10-14).

Theories about the future life, which do not serve this purpose, are best avoided.

Section II. Life after death

1 *Death is not the end of human existence*

  (a) *Death is the separation of the spirit from the body* (2 Corinthians 5:8). The body decays while the spirit lives on, free from human limitations (see section IV).

  (b) *This truth has been clearly made known by the Christian gospel.* Throughout history people have felt sure that death is not the end. They feel that life has meaning for the present and the future and that goodness will finally triumph.

  Christian revelation supports these feelings and shows to all of us our relation to God, to the after-life and to eternity.

  Jesus has 'brought life and immortality to light through the gospel' (2 Timothy 1:10) and by this teaching gave:

   (i) *warning to the sinner* (Mark 8:36, 37; Luke 12:13-21);

   (ii) *comfort to the dying* (Luke 23:43);

   (iii) *consolation for His followers* (John 14:1-3; Matthew 5:11, 12; 10:28; John 11:25, 26);

   (iv) *encouragement to godly living* (Luke 18:28, 30; Mark 13:32-37; Matthew 25:14-30).

  The truth about life after death is an important part of the gospel. Jesus died for our spiritual welfare in this life as well as in the next (John 3:14-16; 6:47-51).

2 *The Bible says nothing about salvation being possible after death, but warns of the danger of dying in sin* (John 8:21)

The story of the rich man and Lazarus (Luke 16:19-31) and the reference to Moses and Elijah on the mountain (Luke 9:30, 31) show that we shall still be our real selves after death and will be able to think, act and remember. We also know that the godly are welcomed by the Lord while the ungodly are sent away from His presence. This is a comfort to the righteous (2 Corinthians 5:8; Philippians 1:23; Revelation 14:13) but a warning to the sinful (Matthew 25:46).

Section III. 'The day of the Lord'

1　*The resurrection of the dead and the judgment spoken of in Article 11 will mark the establishment of God's everlasting Kingdom*

In the Bible this is called:

'the last day' (John 6:39),
'the day of the Lord' (1 Thessalonians 5:2; 2 Peter 3:10),
'the coming of the Lord' (James 5:7),
'the appearing of Jesus Christ' (1 Peter 1:7) and
'the revelation of Jesus Christ' (1 Peter 1:13).

The use of the word 'day' in this way means God's chosen time when His full and final purpose for all creation will be realized.

2　*'The day of the Lord' will also be 'the day of our Lord Jesus Christ'* (1 Corinthians 1:8)

(See also 2 Corinthians 1:14; Philippians 1:6, 10; 2:16.)

Jesus, who on earth took the form of a servant (Philippians 2:7), will show Himself 'in the glory of his Father' (Mark 8:38) and will be seen 'as he is' (1 John 3:2).

3 *It will be a 'day of redemption'* (Ephesians 4:30)
when the full effect of His redeeming work will be
realized (John 14:2, 3; Hebrews 9:28, *New English
Bible*).

4 *It will be a day of resurrection and judgment* (John
5:28, 29).
This will be the time when Christ will judge all mankind
(see Acts 17:31; Romans 2:16; John 5:22; 2 Timothy
4:1).

5 *It will be a day of triumph and great change*
The Lord Jesus Christ will rule in power over all, including His enemies (Hebrews 10:12, 13) and nothing
which is against the will of God will be able to harm His
Kingdom.

The state of mankind and of the whole creation will
be changed. There will be 'a new heaven and a new
earth'. This great change is best described in the words
of the Bible (see Mark 13:31; 2 Peter 3:10, 13; Psalm
102:25-27; Revelation 21:1, 5; 1 Corinthians 15:24,
25, 28).

6 *The Bible has many references to the time of Christ's
coming and to what will happen at the end of this age,
but these are understood in different ways*
This is not surprising seeing that picture language is
sometimes used and little or nothing is said about some
things we would like to understand.

The Salvation Army does not claim to know all the
answers, but calls attention to those Christian truths
affecting life and conduct of which we are sure.

We believe that we should live:

(a) in hope and expectancy, being sure of Christ's

111

final victory (Philippians 2:9-11; Revelation 11:15);

(b) *in holiness,* living the new life we have received and serving as God wills;

(c) *in watchfulness,* always responding to the challenge of knowing that Christ will come (Luke 12:35-40; Romans 14:7-13; Titus 2:12-14; 2 Peter 3:14; 1 John 2:28).

Section IV. The resurrection of the body

1   *This applies to all mankind* (John 5:25-29; Romans 14:9)

2   *The resurrection of the body means something greater than restoring earthly life to the dead*

It is resurrection to a different kind of life when a new 'spiritual body' takes the place of our 'natural body'. Unlike the old body, this new body is not limited by space and time and will never decay (1 Corinthians 15:42-44; 52-54).

Jesus restored life to the daughter of Jairus, to a widow's son and to Lazarus of Bethany. But this was a return to earthly life and they died again in course of time. In raising the dead on earth Jesus proved that He had authority and power to do so.

But His own resurrection was of a different quality by which He fought and conquered the power of death. This victory was won not only for Himself (Acts 2:24; Romans 6:9) but for all mankind (1 Corinthians 15:54).

In this sense He is 'the first fruits of the harvest of the dead' (1 Corinthians 15:20, *New English Bible*) and 'the firstborn from the dead' (Colossians 1:18). Because He rose, we too may rise and may share His risen life.

3 *The New Testament tells of the happy state of those
who are risen and united to Christ as Saviour*

Their victory will be not only over death but over sin
and all its effects. They will be changed into the likeness
of Christ (Romans 8:28, 30; 2 Corinthians 4:16, 17; 5:4,
5; Philippians 3:10, 11, 20, 21) and this will complete
their resurrection joy (John 11:25, 26; Romans 8:10, 11;
Ephesians 1:19, 20).

Section V. The time of judgment for all

'It is appointed unto men once to die, but after this the
judgment' (Hebrews 9:27).

1 *The Bible, in many places, speaks of this coming
judgment at the end of the world*

References are found in the teachings of Jesus (eg
Matthew 13:40-43, 47-50; 16:27; 25:31, 32; Luke 13:24-
30); in the teachings of Peter (Acts 10:42), Paul (Acts
17:31), Jude (14, 15) and John (Revelation 20:12, 13;
22:12).

2 *These references teach that this judgment will be
part of the act of God when His Kingdom will come*

They also show that God's rule over all creation will
mean that there will be no place for anything that is
against the righteous and holy nature of His Kingdom.

3 *Judgment 'at the end of the world' does not mean
that everyone will be facing God's judgment for the
first time*

The Bible shows, from Genesis onwards, that people
and nations are continually being judged by God

(Jeremiah 17:10), a subject given an important place in the messages of the prophets.

Verses in Matthew 24, Mark 13 and Luke 21 speak of God's judgment in this life as well as to the final judgment which will explain all other judgments.

4 *God's judgments are not only concerned with reward or condemnation.*
God as Righteous Judge will speak with comfort and reward to all who have suffered injustice at the hands of their fellow men, especially to those who have suffered for righteousness' sake (Matthew 5:11, 12; Luke 18:7, 8; with Revelation 6:9, 10; 7:14-17).

5 *Final judgment will be with Jesus Christ as Judge* (Matthew 25:31, 32) (see section III, paragraph 4).
This is because, as God, He knows everything and, as man, He shares our human nature (John 5:22, 23, 27).

6 *The day of judgment will be a time of revelation and of giving account of our earthly living*
  (a) *The truth about all things will be made known* and everyone will be judged in this light (1 Corinthians 3:13).
  (b) *We shall all learn the truth about ourselves* (Romans 2:16; 1 Corinthians 4:5) *and also the truth about the purposes and power of God.*
  (c) *We will see ourselves as God sees us, all things being known and understood* (1 Corinthians 13:12).
   Thus divine judgment will be a fair judgment, taking into account each person's understanding and opportunity (Matthew 11:21-24; Luke 12:48).
  (d) *The value of human deeds will be made known.*

All actions will be seen in the light of their *eternal value* (1 Corinthians 3:13) and their *final effect* for good or ill.

(e) *All who have heard of Jesus will be judged in the light of this privilege and responsibility* (John 12:48; Luke 12:8, 9).

(f) We will be judged according to what we have done (2 Corinthians 5:10) or failed to do (Matthew 25:24-30). (See also Matthew 16:26; Romans 2:6-9; Revelation 22:12.)

Section VI. The eternal happiness of the righteous

1   *The righteous will be happy for ever because:*

(a) *they will be with God for ever, in whose presence is 'fullness of joy'* (1 Thessalonians 4:17; Psalm 16:11);

(b) *Heaven will be a perfect place for them because they have been made ready for it;*

(c) *they will find joy in the redeeming grace that has made them fit for God's presence and brought them there* (John 14:3; Revelation 5:9, 10).

2   *The word 'heaven' is used in the Bible with at least two separate meanings*

(a) *To describe the space beyond the earth* (Genesis 1:1).

This is the heaven which, with the earth, will pass away (Matthew 24:35; 2 Peter 3:7, 10; Revelation 6:14). There will be a new heaven and a new earth (2 Peter 3:13; Revelation 21:1) which means a new kind of life.

(b) *To define the eternal dwelling place of God where His redeemed children also will live.*

It is in this sense that Jesus spoke of the Father who is in Heaven (Matthew 5:16; 6:9; 16:17; 23:9) and of Himself as having come from Heaven (John 3:12, 13; 6:33, 38, 42). He also spoke of Heaven as being the eternal home of God's children (Matthew 5:12; 6:20; John 14:2).

New Testament writers say that the ascended Lord Jesus is now in Heaven (Ephesians 6:9; Colossians 4:1; Hebrews 9:24; 1 Peter 3:22).

3　*For the righteous Heaven will be a state of great blessedness* (see Romans 8:18, *New English Bible*).

Bible writers were inspired to use much picture language in trying to describe the blessedness of Heaven (eg Revelation 21 and 22). Yet the real experience will be greater than the picture.

4　*Life in Heaven will be full of joy because:*

(a) *God's Kingdom will, in its full glory, be freed from all that is impure or imperfect* (Revelation 21:4, 5; 7:16; 22:3; 21:27).

(b) *The full purpose of God's redeeming grace will be realized.*

The greatest joy of the righteous will come from their new and full relationship with their Lord and Redeemer. They will be united with Him in spirit and so be changed into His likeness (Philippians 3:20, 21; 1 John 3:2; John 17:23, 24).

(c) *God's children will be fulfilling the purpose for which they were created.*

They will have the highest privilege of serving God in His presence for ever (Revelation 7:15, 22:3, 4).

(d) *There will still be growth and progress in Heaven.* Jesus taught that faithful servants are given more opportunities to use the powers which they develop by work that is well done (Matthew 25:14-30; Luke 19:11-27).

(e) *The joys of Heaven will last for ever* (1 Peter 1:4).

Section VII. The endless punishment of the wicked

1 *This endless punishment is that the unrighteous are separated from God's presence and suffer the results of this separation*

Jesus warned of this in His teaching which spoke of 'everlasting punishment' (Matthew 25:46).

2 *This suffering and loss is spoken of in many ways and mostly in picture language* (see Matthew 8:12; 25:30; Mark 9:43; Matthew 13:42, 50)

The unrighteous are likened to guests shut out from the feast (Matthew 25:10, 11) and to things that are burned or cast away (Matthew 13:30, 48).

Other New Testament words used to describe this state are *destruction* (Matthew 7:13), *perdition,* meaning ruin (Revelation 17:11), *to perish* (John 3:16), the *second death* (Revelation 2:11; 21:8) and *hell* (Matthew 10:28; 23:15, 33).

3 *To be sent away from God's presence is the most serious form of punishment*

This is the 'second death' or the final result of that separation from God which began on earth. It is the opposite of the 'eternal life' Jesus promised to those who accept Him as Saviour (see Matthew 25:41, 34).

4 *The Bible contrasts the sad fate of the unrighteous with the reward of the righteous and says that both are eternal*

The word translated as 'eternal' or 'everlasting' has two meanings: *(a)* that which never ends and *(b)* that which belongs to a new and different quality of life. Both these meanings apply to life after death.

The Bible does not teach, as some say, that the unrighteous will cease to exist or that they can hope for release from their fate in the afterlife.

5 *The final state of the unrighteous has been decided by their own choice*

(a) *This is the result of their refusing to accept the gospel and all influences for their good* (John 3:18, 19).

(b) *Their punishment is not in keeping with God's will and loving purpose which is to save and change them* (John 3:17).

God created us to live in fellowship with Him and to be like Him. He planned our salvation at great cost (John 3:16; 1 John 4:14).

(c) *The tragedy of hell is possible because God has made us all free to choose whether we will live with Him or separate ourselves from Him.*

God will not take away this freedom nor cancel its effects.

Appendix I. The Salvation Army and the sacraments

One way in which The Salvation Army is different from most other Churches is that it does not practise sacraments in its worship. Sacraments are fixed ceremonies or rituals, and most Protestant Churches practice two of them—baptism and holy communion (or the Lord's supper)—though the Roman Catholic Church recognizes seven sacraments.

The Army does not deny that other Christians receive blessing or grace from God by these means, but it does say that they are only outward *signs* of inner spiritual experience. We Salvationists may use other signs—for example, kneeling at the Penitent-form, or having our children dedicated under the flag—but we do not *have* to use any of these signs in order to worship properly or to know salvation from sin. John 4:24 makes it clear that what *is* necessary is that we should worship 'in spirit and in truth'; this means that we should have a knowledge of God's presence in our inner selves, and a desire to find the truth in Him.

Many Christians believe that Jesus commanded the use of the sacraments by all Christians in all ages. If this were so, we would have to use them. But in fact the New Testament does not speak of them as essential, and there is nothing to substantiate the fact that Jesus or even the leaders of the Early Church meant them to become fixed ceremonies for ever.

Salvationists, therefore, are not just seeking to be different, and though they do not use these signs, they must seek all the more for the real spiritual experience to which they point.

119

Baptism in water

Up to the time of John the Baptist it was usual for non-Jews who wished to become Jews to be baptized (dipped in water) as a sign of conversion. John the Baptist called on the *Jews* themselves to be baptized as a sign of turning away from sin (repentance). He told them that they would not get into God's Kingdom just because they were Jews (children of Abraham) (Matthew 3:1, 2, 5-9).

John clearly said that his water baptism would be replaced by a greater and more spiritual baptism (Matthew 3:11; John 1:29-33).

What did Jesus do?

When Jesus was ready to begin His work for God, He showed that He agreed with John's call for the nation to repent by being baptized Himself (Matthew 3:13-17). The words 'for the present' and 'conform' (Matthew 3:15, *New English Bible*) suggest, however, that Jesus did not mean baptism to be a custom which would continue for ever.

In John 3:22, 23 it is said that Jesus Himself baptized people, but from John 4:1, 2 we learn that, in fact, only His disciples baptized. When Jesus sent His disciples out on missions He did not tell them to baptize and there is no record that they did (Matthew 10:1 to 11:1; Luke 10:1-20).

What did Jesus say?

When Jesus spoke of 'baptism' He did not always mean water baptism. He sometimes used the word to describe any experience which makes one 'a different man'—for example, Mark 10:38, 39; Luke 12:50.

It is often thought that there are three places in the Gospels where Jesus was commanding baptism, but there are good reasons for believing that these are not actually commands of Jesus to baptize in water.

(a) 'Born from water' in John 3:5 probably does not mean baptism at all, but physical birth, which is referred to in verses 4 and 6. (In verse 8 water is not mentioned.)

(b) Mark 16:16 was probably not part of Mark's Gospel as it was first written. Many scholars believe that it was added later and shows the ideas of some people in the Early Church. In any case *water* is not mentioned. 'Baptism' could refer to the baptism of the Holy Spirit.

(c) The third reference is Matthew 28:19. Here again it seems that the words 'in the name of the Father and the Son and the Holy Spirit' were not used until long after the time of Jesus. In Acts (eg, 10:48, *New English Bible*) the words used at baptism are 'in the name of Jesus Christ'. Again the word *water* is not used so that even if these *were* the actual words of Jesus they could still refer to the spiritual experience of baptism in the Holy Spirit.

The New Testament Church

Without doubt the custom of water baptism continued into the Early Church, but as a *sign* of new life in Christ, not as something necessary to create that new life. Wherever water baptism and Holy Spirit baptism are spoken of together they either mean the same, or Holy Spirit baptism is clearly shown to be the more important (Acts 1:5; 2:38; 8:13-17). It is clear that water baptism, as John the Baptist had used it, was not thought to be enough (Acts 11:15, 16; 18:24-26; 19:1-7). Holy Spirit baptism *was* necessary.

In the Epistles, Hebrews 6:1-3 speaks of water

baptism, but only as something from which we should go on to full growth. Paul discouraged water baptism and himself rarely baptized, at least at Corinth (1 Corinthians 1:10-17).

Several Epistles use the word 'baptism' to mean a spiritual experience, not an outward ceremony (Romans 6:3, 4; 1 Corinthians 12:13; Galatians 3:27; Colossians 2:12; 1 Peter 3:21, 22), and Romans 8:9 and Ephesians 1:13 clearly show that Holy Spirit baptism is what makes a Christian.

Holy communion or the Lord's supper

This is based on the last meal Jesus had with His disciples, which was probably the annual Passover meal, when Jews remembered their ancestors' escape from slavery in Egypt (the Exodus). Cakes of bread baked without yeast were shared (eg, Matthew 26:26), and four cups of wine were passed round (Matthew 26:27-29).

The Christian ceremony is based on the story as told only by Luke (22:19, 20), but it should be clearly noted that in the oldest copies of this Gospel, this passage ends at 'This is my body . . .' and the words 'Do this as a memorial of Me' are not there. They have been added at a later date and some modern translations leave them out. If Jesus really did give this command, it is very unlikely that it would have been left out, for example, of Mark's Gospel, for it is thought that Peter supplied most of the information given in that Gospel.

John's Gospel does not mention the sharing of bread and wine at all, but tells the story of Jesus washing the disciples' feet, including the very clear command of Jesus, 'You also ought to wash one another's feet' (John 13:14). Many Christians place great importance on a doubtful command ('Do this as a memorial of Me')

122

and yet take no notice of the very clear command about the washing of feet.

The 'common meal'

In the Acts of the Apostles there is no record of a *ceremonial* meal, though there are references to the disciples eating full meals together (2:42; 20:7, 11) as part of their sharing of all that they owned (2:44, 45; 4:32). If Jesus had so recently commanded the disciples to hold a special ceremony to remember Him by, it is very surprising that in the Acts of the Apostles, which deals with the work of the two main leaders of the Early Church (Peter and Paul), and which was written by the same author as Luke's Gospel, there is no mention of the command being obeyed.

In 1 Corinthians 11:24 (which was almost certainly written before the Gospels) the doubtful command from Luke 22:19, 20 is seen again, but the background to this chapter probably suggests how the ceremonial meal first came to be held. In verses 17-34 it is clear that the Corinthian Christians were making the common meal an *eating* occasion rather than a worshipping occasion. Some were having more than enough while others almost starved, and some were even getting drunk (verses 20, 21).

To put these matters right, Paul suggested a new attitude to the common meal which would show that it should give *spiritual* food rather than food for the *body*. Because of this the meal became more of a ceremony.

This move away from *things* to *meanings* leads naturally to our way of thinking, where we do not use the *things* (bread and wine) at all, but seek for the spiritual experience. Paul himself condemned those who failed to recognize the *meaning* of the ceremony (1 Corinthians 11:29).

As time went on the ceremony and the meal were separated. By the beginning of the second century AD, Christians met early on Sunday for the ceremony and later in the day for a full fellowship meal. Eventually, common (or fellowship) meals were forbidden and only the ceremony was held.

There is a strange but complete silence in large sections of the New Testament about this ceremony, which is thought by many to have been commanded by Jesus. There is no mention of it in Romans, Galatians, Ephesians, Philippians, Colossians, 1 and 2 Timothy and Titus (which are about church procedure), Hebrews, James, 1 and 2 Peter, 1, 2 and 3 John, Jude and Revelation. This suggests that it cannot have been thought to be necessary in New Testament times.

Salvationists, therefore, think that there is little or no proof that either Jesus or the New Testament Church leaders commanded a ritual meal to be held by all Christians for all time. However, though we do not observe the ceremony of holy communion, we must constantly seek for God's spiritual gifts, that is for full communion with Him and willingness to be used in the service of others.

> My life must be Christ's broken bread,
> My love His outpoured wine,
> A cup o'erfilled, a table spread
> Beneath His name and sign,
> That other souls, refreshed and fed,
> May share His life through mine.
>
> (Albert Orsborn)

Religious ceremonies

There is no doubt that spiritual blessing can come to us through the ceremonies which may be part of our worship. There is always the danger, however, of the spiritual meaning of the ceremony being forgotten. The Old Testament has many examples of people losing touch with the Spirit of God, although they were very carefully carrying out the details of the Law's demands.

In His time, Jesus had to condemn the religious leaders for this dependence on outward forms without inward holiness (Matthew 5:17-48; 12:1-13; 22:34-40; 23:1-39; Mark 7:1-23). It seems unlikely that He would have commanded new ceremonies with the same danger.

In Acts 15 (especially verses 28 and 29) the list of things which the Jerusalem Church (under the guidance of the Holy Spirit) thought necessary does not include any ceremonies.

The Epistle to the Hebrews clearly teaches that Jewish ceremonies are replaced in the Christian Church by spiritual blessings (see 7:23-28; 8:7-13; 9:1-15, 24, 27, 28; 10:1-6, 11-14, 19-22).

Is there, therefore, any good reason for ending circumcision and the Passover meal, only to replace them with baptism and holy communion? For the most part Salvationists would think that there is not.

See for reference other Salvation Army literature such as *Closer Communion* (Clifford Kew) and *The Salvationist and the Sacraments* (Wm Metcalf).

Appendix II. The Apostles' Creed

I believe in God the Father almighty, Maker of heaven and earth:

And in Jesus Christ His only Son our Lord, who was conceived by the Holy Ghost, born of the Virgin Mary, suffered under Pontius Pilate, was crucified, dead and buried; He descended into hell; the third day He rose again from the dead. He ascended into heaven, and sitteth on the right hand of God the Father almighty; from thence He shall come to judge the quick and the dead.

I believe in the Holy Ghost, the holy catholic Church, the communion of saints, the forgiveness of sins, the resurrection of the body, and the life everlasting.

Appendix III. The Nicene Creed

I believe in one God the Father almighty, Maker of heaven and earth, and of all things visible and invisible;

And in one Lord Jesus Christ, the only-begotten Son of God, begotten of His Father before all worlds, God of God, Light of Light, very God of very God, begotten, not made, being of one substance with the Father, by whom all things were made:

Who for us men and for our salvation came down from heaven, and was incarnate by the Holy Ghost of the Virgin Mary, and was made man, and was crucified also for us under Pontius Pilate. He suffered and was buried, and the third day He rose again according to the Scriptures, and ascended into heaven, and sitteth on the right hand of the Father. And He shall come again with glory to judge both the quick and the dead; whose kingdom shall have no end.

And I believe in the Holy Ghost, the Lord and Giver of life, who proceedeth from the Father and the Son, who with the Father and the Son together is worshipped and glorified, who spake by the prophets.

And I believe in one catholic and apostolic Church. I acknowledge one baptism for the remission of sins. And I look for the resurrection of the dead, and the life of the world to come.

Glossary

Some words that will be found in Bible or doctrine studies, along with their meanings.

ADOPTION
God's acceptance of the forgiven sinner as His child.

ASCENSION
The departure of Christ's visible presence from earth to return to His former power and glory (Mark 16:19; Luke 24:51; Acts 1:9).

ASSURANCE
The sure knowledge God gives to believers that they have been forgiven and accepted by Him (see 'Witness').

ATONEMENT
Being made at one or at peace with God (Romans 5:10).

ATTRIBUTE
A quality of character. The attributes of God are the special qualities which are part of His divine nature.

CHRIST
The name or title given to Jesus in the Bible and meaning Messiah or 'Anointed' or 'Chosen One' (John 1:41).

CONVERSION
The change brought about by the Holy Spirit in a person resulting from repentance for sins and saving faith in Jesus.

COVENANT
A binding agreement such as that which God makes with His people (Genesis 9:16).

128

CREATOR — One who brings into being something out of nothing. This is one of God's titles (see Genesis 1:1; Isaiah 40:28).

DEITY — Another word for God.

DIVINE — Coming from, belonging to, or being like God.

ETERNAL — That which always was or always will be (everlasting). Can also describe the quality of new life in Christ.

FINITE — Limited. Not infinite.

GODHEAD — God in His supremacy.

GOVERNOR — One who rules with authority. Thus God is Governor of all things (Psalm 22:28).

GRACE — The undeserved love of God towards the sinner, including the mercy which forgives him. Grace enables him to live a Christlike life.

HOLINESS — Christlike character, the complete work of grace that God desires to bring about in human lives (see SANCTIFICATION).

HUMAN — Coming from, belonging to, or being like man.

INCARNATION — Being 'made flesh' or becoming human—the union of the divine and human natures in the Person of Jesus Christ.

INFINITE — Without limit—not finite.

JUDGMENT

The event when God will require each person to account for his attitude and action during his earthly life.

JUSTIFICATION

Being declared just or right in the sight of God because He in Christ has forgiven the repentant sinner.

MESSIAH

The name or title given to Jesus in the Bible and meaning 'Anointed One' or 'Chosen One' (see CHRIST).

MORAL

That which has to do with human behaviour, especially with the knowledge of right and wrong.

OMNIPOTENT

All-powerful. Attribute of God.

OMNIPRESENT

Present everywhere. Attribute of God.

OMNISCIENT

Knowing everything. Attribute of God.

PRESERVER

One who protects and sustains. Thus God, as Preserver, provides and cares for all He has created.

REDEMPTION

Being made free from the slavery of sin through faith in Christ (1 Corinthians 6:20).

RENUNCIATION

Giving up or turning away from something (Mark 8:34).

RESURRECTION

The rising to life of that which was dead. The historical fact that Christ rose from the dead. The quality of life His followers will share by His promise.

REVELATION
The making known of that which otherwise would remain unknown or hidden.

SALVATION
Being saved from the guilt and final effects of sin through faith in Christ.

SANCTIFICATION
Set apart and kept for God's service. The process whereby one is made holy (see HOLINESS).

SUPERNATURAL
That which is not of the natural world or subject to the known laws of nature.

TRADITION
In the Bible, tradition usually means rules or practices passed down over many years and refers to the early spoken or unwritten laws of the Jews. Jesus condemned the abuse of these (Matthew 15:3, 6; Mark 7:5, 9, 13). Church tradition means that which has become the custom in belief, worship etc.

TRINITY
The unity of the three Persons of the Godhead—Father, Son and Holy Spirit.

UNIVERSE
All of God's creation—all worlds and all that exists.

WITNESS
The assurance given by the Holy Spirit to the believer that he is accepted by God. Also the act of people making known to others what they have seen or experienced.

Subject index

Subject index

Subject index

GRACE
  definition 129
  holiness a work of 96

HEAVEN
  definition 115
  joy of 115-117

HELL
  definition 117
  tragedy of 118

HOLINESS (see also SANCTIFICATION)
  crisis and process 101
  God and 13, 92-94
  grace and 96
  Holy Spirit and 97, 98
  Jesus and 30, 96, 101
  source of 93

HOLY SPIRIT
  adoption, witness of 83
  attributes of 37, 38
  Christian Church and 41, 42
  disobedience against 38
  enabling believers 39, 71
  gifts of 42
  Jesus and 39
  inspiration of the Bible and 6
  inward working of 86
  obedience to 86
  Old Testament days and 39
  Person, a 38
  presence of 40
  regeneration by 79-81